THE BEST OF BROCHURE DESIGN 10

PERRY CHUA

BEVERLY MASSACHUSETTS

ROCKPORT PUBLISHERS

CONTENTS

First published in the United States of America by
Rockport Publishers, a member of
Quayside Publishing Group
100 Cummings Center
Suite 406-L
Beverly, Massachusetts 01915-6101
Telephone: (978) 282-9590
Fax: (978) 283-2742
www.rockpub.com

Library of Congress Cataloging-in-Publication Data
Chua, Perry.
The best of brochure design 10 / Perry Chua.
   p.   cm.
   ISBN 978-1-59253-446-3
   1. Brochures--Design. I. Title. II. Title: Best of brochure design ten.
Z246.5.B76C48 2008
686--dc22

                                        2008023505
                                             CIP

© 2008 by Rockport Publishers, Inc.

ISBN-13: 978-1-59253-446-3
ISBN-10: 1-59253-446-5

10 9 8 7 6 5 4 3 2 1

Design
Perry Chua
perrychua.com

Production
Jason Pavich - Manager
Simon West - Assistant

Photography
Thomas Billingsley
thomasbillingsley.com

Cover Illustration
Adrien Van Viersen

Printed in Singapore

PREFACE

Can you judge a brochure by its cover? Well, yes, you often can.

A brochure is a lot like a person. Each is different; every one has something to say. The brochure cover, for example, has to do a good job of introducing itself, as if to say, "You might want to listen to this and here's why." If the cover can compel the reader to pick it up and open it, a major hurdle has been overcome.

Next comes the chance to communicate. Through pictures and words—and everything in between— the brochure tells its story to the reader compellingly and with relevance. It should hold their interest until they are ready to do, think, or even feel what you want them to.

The selected entries featured here were judged on many different levels, among them effective use of typography, design, and craftsmanship. But, like the hallmarks of any successful brochure, winning entries hold one thing in common: outstanding pick-up appeal. And like a good book, we found them impossible to put down. Each virtually jumped into our hands and drove us to explore page by page, line by line, and image by image. And every one had its own story to tell.

At times, I have feared that the printed brochure would be to the digital age what the horse and cart was to the automobile. But, in reviewing submissions from around the globe, I became convinced of the staying power of good design on paper. Far from a selection of "paper salesmen," what you see in these pages is an integral part of a design system—one that allows the expression of brand vision by eloquently articulating brand character.

To all those who contributed, I offer congratulations and a heartfelt thank you. You made this book possible. With over 1400 entries received from 28 countries, some 200 entries were selected for inclusion. I am truly honored to be a part of this remarkable collection of design excellence. I hope you enjoy the outcome as much as I enjoyed the process.

Perry Chua

★ | IN THIS SECTION

DESIGN ARMY

RAMP

DESIGN DEPOT

WECHSLER

CARRÉNOIR ROMA

HANGAR 18 CREATIVE GROUP

PETRICK DESIGN

THE JUPITER DRAWING ROOM

PHILOGRAPHICA, INC.

SALTERBAXTER

ANNUAL REPORTS

★ | **DESIGN ARMY** | ART DIRECTOR **PUM LEFEBURE, JAKE LEFEBURE** | DESIGNER **MIKE MALUSO**
CLIENT **BLACK BOOK PUBLISHING** | PAPER/MATERIALS **FINCH FINE**

DESIGN ARMY | ART DIRECTOR **PUM LEFEBURE, JAKE LEFEBURE** | DESIGNER **MIKE MALUSO** ★
CLIENT **BLACK BOOK PUBLISHING** | PAPER/MATERIALS **FINCH FINE**

USA

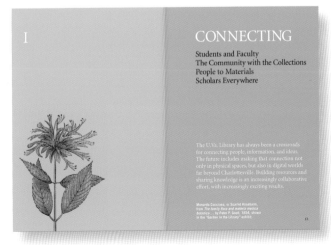

(Opposite page) Letter from Thomas Jefferson to Peter S. DuPonceau, 28 December 1820, from the Albert H. Small Declaration of Independence Collection

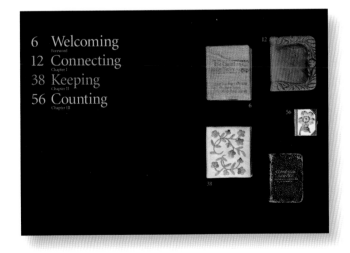

I CONNECTING

Students and Faculty
The Community with the Collections
People to Materials
Scholars Everywhere

The U.Va. Library has always been a crossroads for connecting people, information, and ideas. The future includes making that connection not only in physical spaces, but also in digital worlds far beyond Charlottesville. Building resources and sharing knowledge is an increasingly collaborative effort, with increasingly exciting results.

Monarda Coccinea, or Scarlet Rosebalm, from The family flora and materia medica Botanica ... by Peter P. Good, 1854, shown in the "Garden in the Library" exhibit.

★ **RAMP** | ART DIRECTOR **MICHAEL STINSON** | DESIGNER **CLAIRE DE LÉON, ANGELA KIM**
CLIENT **CWS CAPITAL PARTNERS, LLC** | PAPER/MATERIALS **WEYERHAEUSER COUGAR OPAQUE VELLUM 80 LB. TEXT**

Circulate Or Die

GARY CARMELL   PRESIDENT

I was in the checkout line in Barnes & Noble and I noticed the discount book bin as I was waiting. The first book to catch my eye was about reflexology, a special type of hand and foot massage. To pass the time I picked up the book and started leafing through it. The first thing I saw when I opened it up was a quote that said, "Circulation is life." It was such a simple statement yet so profound in that it goes way beyond its obvious application to health, and it caused me to immediately think about it in the context of investing and CWS.

What I've learned over the years in our business is we always have to keep moving forward and circulate our capital in ways that ensure we are aligning our management capabilities with the best opportunities available. This does not necessarily mean we always have to be buying and selling. On the contrary, it may mean sticking with investments that we believe offer an outstanding risk/reward relationship for a long period of time. To ensure that we extract the maximum value from the investment we must make sure that we are circulating our talent, capital, and residents so that we are attracting the best customer base capable of paying what we hope will be growing rents.

Since change is the one constant we can rely on as a result of the shifting winds of economic conditions, demographic forces, and the risk appetite of investors, standing still is not a viable option. These forces may require us to make more significant changes by altering geographic emphasis or even the types of properties we purchase or develop.

The history of CWS is one of a company that has been nimble and flexible in making significant strategic moves over the last 30-plus years to make certain that we are capturing the opportunities that we believe offer the best risk/reward relationship.

The very first investment that CWS made was an apartment building in Huntington Beach and after that we gravitated to manufactured housing communities which were known as mobile home parks back then.

We grew the mobile home park business fairly aggressively over a 20-year period as evidenced by CWS becoming one of the largest owners and operators of mobile home parks in the country. At our peak, we operated in nine states, including both coasts, and in Canada.

As our sophistication grew and capabilities strengthened, we shifted to more value-added opportunities by developing, expanding, and redeveloping communities as well as turning around problem properties brought about by unprecedented economic turmoil experienced in Texas after the price of oil collapsed and large numbers of S&Ls failed.

We realized that at the same time that we were dealing with challenges in our mobile home park portfolio, there were tremendous opportunities developing in the tumultuous apartment industry with the creation of the Resolution Trust Corporation, or the RTC, as it was better known.

We put together a team of focused people to exploit the innumerable opportunities to buy foreclosed properties from insurance companies, the RTC, and banks because we thought that the risk/reward was extraordinary. To capitalize these opportunities, we started recirculating money from our California mobile home parks in the late 1990's because we saw that conditions in California were top dead center in the sense that prices were extremely high and the fundamentals going forward were very much at risk as defense spending was contracting and a large number of high paying jobs were going to be lost. When this was combined with California's high cost of living and relatively anti-business climate, we were quite bearish on California real estate, particularly housing prices.

We moved capital from mobile home parks that we sold in California and reinvested this money in depressed assets in Texas and did quite well on our investments there.

In addition, once we saw that the apartment industry was starting to gain traction and many of the markets that we were in were stopping new development because money was not available, vacancy rates were too high, and rents were too low to support new construction, we realized that over time there would be an opportunity to create new apartment communities that would be in high demand.

In the early 1990's, we started developing some of the modern class A apartment communities which had far more amenities and

USA

LETTER TO THE INVESTORS

Nº 2006

5

WRITTEN BY THE CWS

FIVE PARTNERS

STEVEN J. SH[...]

0414197605   Annual Report

Real Estate Investment Specialists

Newport Beach

CREATED CIRCA 1969

CWS CAPITAL PARTNERS · CIRCULATING VALUE · EST. 1969

MMVI

President   Chief Executive Officer

2006 × 2006 × 2006 × 2006 × 2006 × 2006 × 2006 × 2006 × 2006 × 2006 × 2006 × 2006

★ **DESIGN DEPOT** | ART DIRECTOR **BANKOV PITER** | DESIGNER **EUGENY MALYSHEV** | CLIENT **SOGAZ**

RUSSIA

WECHSLER | ART DIRECTOR **MIKE HALL** | DESIGNER **MIKE HALL, SUE ROBERTSON** | CLIENT **ARCAPITA** ★
PAPER/MATERIALS **IKONO SILK**

UNITED KINGDOM

★ | **CARRÉNOIR ROMA** | ART DIRECTOR **MASSIMILIANO SAGRATI** | DESIGNER **ALFREDO LANEVE**
CLIENT **FINMECCANICA**

★ **HANGAR 18 CREATIVE GROUP** | ART DIRECTOR **KIM WOLF** | DESIGNER **KIM WOLF**
CLIENT **VANCOUVER INTERNATIONAL AIRPORT**

CANADA

PETRICK DESIGN | ART DIRECTOR **ROBERT PETRICK** | DESIGNER **JEF ANDERSON** | CLIENT **COVANTA HOLDING CORP.**
PAPER/MATERIALS **NEENAH ENVIRONMENT PC100–WHITE, SMOOTH 80 LB. COVER AND 100 LB. TEXT, WRAP: CT1, GLAMA NATURAL RECYCLED, 36 LB.**

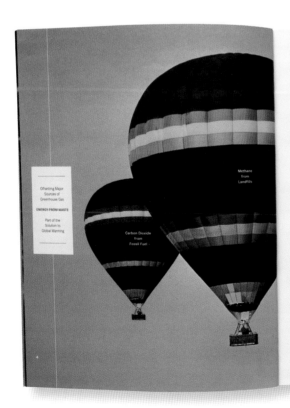

USA

★ | **THE JUPITER DRAWING ROOM** | DESIGNER **ASHRAF MAJIE, WASEEMA SURHADIA** | CLIENT **SANLAM**
PAPER/MATERIALS **AVALON MATTE**

SOUTH AFRICA

USA

★ | **RAMP** | ART DIRECTOR **RACHEL ELNAR, MICHAEL STINSON** | DESIGNER **CLAIRE DE LÉON**
CLIENT **EDWARDS LIFESCIENCES** | PAPER/MATERIALS **WEYERHAEUSER COUGAR OPAQUE**

USA

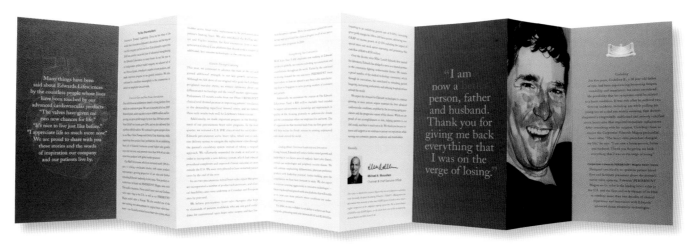

SALTERBAXTER | ART DIRECTOR **JAMES WILSON** | DESIGNER **ALAN DELGADO**
CLIENT **ERNST & YOUNG** | PAPER/MATERIALS **REVIVE** | ★

UNITED KINGDOM

Our profession continues to change, but today we have a clear picture of where it is going and how we must adapt – and our achievements this year demonstrate this. The business world as a whole has adjusted well to the increased economic and political uncertainties of the past several years and demand for the quality services that we provide has been high.

In the UK, during our 2004-2005 financial year, each of our service lines grew and we increased our overall gross fee income by 15%, to £945m, with an average profit per partner of £561k.

On the following two pages I answer some of the most important questions Ernst & Young faces.

★ | **SALTERBAXTER** | ART DIRECTOR **JAMES WILSON** | DESIGNER **ROSE TOMLINSON** | CLIENT **LAND SECURITIES**
PAPER/MATERIALS **CHALLENGER OFFSET**

UNITED KINGDOM

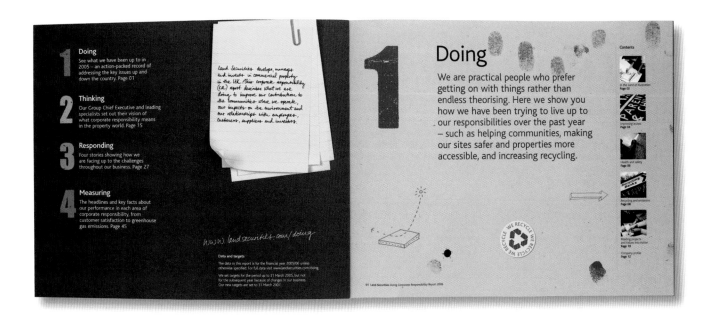

SALTERBAXTER | ART DIRECTOR **JAMES WILSON** | DESIGNER **NINA PICKUP** | CLIENT **ALLEN & OVERY** ★
PAPER/MATERIALS **NEPTUNE UNIQUE**

ALLEN & OVERY

[ ]

What it takes...
Annual Report 2007

28
Corporate responsibility

Community

Following our success in two similar cases last year, we
have achieved a significant victory in overturning an
unsafe murder conviction in a Caribbean death row case.

[*Life*]

29
Corporate responsibility

Community

Our Belgium offices work with two local charities
that support hundreds of families across the country
that have lost children through road accidents.

[*Death*]

We are a committed member of the Capital Cases Panel, which
represents, on a pro bono basis, prisoners on death row who wish
to appeal to the Privy Council. On 10 May 2007 the Privy Council
upheld our appeal on behalf of Wilberforce Bernard, a prisoner
on death row in Trinidad, against his conviction for murder. Their
Lordships ruled that Bernard's conviction was unsafe because of
the inexperience of his counsel at trial in Trinidad, and because the
trial judge failed to give his counsel sufficient opportunity to prepare
his case properly.

Former Allen & Overy litigation associate Richard Hamilton travelled
to Trinidad, after an initial appeal failed, to gather crucial further
evidence that led to the President of Trinidad referring Bernard's
case back to the Court of Appeal in Trinidad. Richard Hamilton
remained involved in the case after leaving Allen & Overy to serve
in the army. When he was tragically killed in a canoeing accident,

the firm remained committed to Bernard's case. In 2007, following
the firm's successful appeal, Allen & Overy litigation associate, James
Freeman, who succeeded Richard Hamilton on the case, was named
'Lawyer of the Week' by The Times newspaper for his contribution to
Bernard's case.

Two more of these rare successes were secured in 2006. In April
we successfully appealed to the Court of Appeal of Jamaica against
the conviction of Garnett Edwards for capital murder, and in February
we won an appeal on behalf of Jamaican death row prisoner
Shabbaddean Peart.

"It is incredibly rewarding work," says Andrew Waters, a litigation
associate who worked on the Bernard case. "There's no doubt that
the day I spoke to Wilberforce once we'd received the judgment goes
down as one of the most momentous in my life."

In Belgium we have a strong connection with two organisations,
OVK-PEVR and Zebra, that support the victims of road accidents
and their families. Brussels-based partner Francis Herbert co-
founded OVK in 1994 with nine other families, following the death
of his daughter who was killed by a drunk driver the previous year.
The association now gives support to over 400 families across
Belgium who have lost children through road accidents. It also
works with agencies across the country tackling road safety issues
and lobbies both local and federal government authorities.

In recent years, OVK has been instrumental in convincing the
Belgian authorities that they should follow the example of countries

such as the UK and the Netherlands in establishing an inventory on
every issue that contributes to road accidents. As a result, actions to
prevent accidents have been implemented and deadlines for progress
established. Since its launch, there has been a 25% reduction
in deaths caused by road accidents in Belgium.

We have supported OVK from its inception. The firm has contributed
financially to the organisation, taken it on as a pro bono client,
provided it with secretarial and logistical support and, for a number
of years, housed its headquarters. Zebra is a Flemish charity that
works closely with OVK, focusing on helping young victims of road
accidents who are left injured and maimed.

Allen & Overy
Annual Report
2007

Allen & Overy
Annual Report
2007

★ IN THIS SECTION

CORPORATE

★ **DESIGN DEPOT** | ART DIRECTOR **BANKOV PITER** | DESIGNER **EUGENY MALYSHEV** | CLIENT **OSTAFYEVO**

CONTENTS

#5

SPACE

perspectives

**ALWAYS
A CLEAR SKY**

We wish you a nice flight and anticipate
to see you in Ostafyevo

RUSSIA

THIS IS WHO WE ARE. OUR GREATEST CAPITAL IS INTELLECTUAL: US.
OUR MINDS AND HOW WE APPLY THEM. TOGETHER, EACH DAY,
TO MAKE OUR CUSTOMERS' NETWORKS OPERATE AT REDUCED RISKS
AND INCREASED OPERATING RATIOS.

MASTERMINDING RAIL TRANSPORTATION.

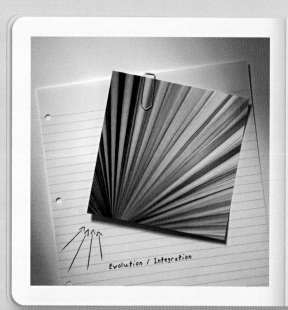

ANSALDO STS REPRESENTS OUR INTEGRATION WORLDWIDE.

OUR SIGNALLING AND TRANSPORT SYSTEMS ACTIVITIES MERGED
TO HELP US WIN MORE CONTRACTS IN A GLOBAL MARKET THAT DEMANDS
A MORE COMPLETE, INTEGRATED, YET LOCAL APPROACH.

CARRÉNOIR ROMA | ART DIRECTOR **MASSIMILIANO SAGRATI** | DESIGNER **EMANUELA CAPPELLI** ‖ ★
CLIENT **ANSALDO STS** | PAPER/MATERIALS **ANTALIS EDITME SOFT WHITE**

★ | **DESIGN ARMY** | ART DIRECTOR **PUM LEFEBURE, JAKE LEFEBURE** | DESIGNER **DAN ADLER** | CLIENT **AMERICAN INSTITUTE OF GRAPHIC ARTS, WASHINGTON DC CHAPTER** | PAPER/MATERIALS **MOHAWK SUPERFINE, FOIL STAMPING**

USA

PAPA INC. | ART DIRECTOR **DUBRAVKO PAPA** | DESIGNER **DUBRAVKO PAPA** | CLIENT **GEOFOTO D.O.O.** | ★
PAPER/MATERIALS **MUNKEN POLAR, ANTISTATIC BAG**

★ **WECHSLER** | ART DIRECTOR **MIKE HALL** | DESIGNER **SUE ROBERTSON, AARON SHAW** | CLIENT **TDR CAPITAL**
PAPER/MATERIALS **NATURALIS AND CURIOUS TRANSLUCENT CLEAR**

UNITED KINGDOM

TDR is a highly selective private equity investment firm with a track record of investing in businesses that have delivered excellent returns for our investors.

When we invest in a business we're investing much more than finance alone – time, knowledge, operational expertise and a pragmatic ability to make things happen are key to creating and capturing value.

THE JUPITER DRAWING ROOM | DESIGNER **BRANDT BOTES** | CLIENT **SANLAM**
PAPER/MATERIALS **MAGNO MATTE AND CROMATICA** | ★

★ **THE JUPITER DRAWING ROOM** | DESIGNER **BRANDT BOTES** | CLIENT **SANLAM**
PAPER/MATERIALS **200 GSM EURO MATTE ART**

SOUTH AFRICA

We find the right partnerships, then set them free.

SMMI's combination analysis allows individual managers to focus on what they do best. For each asset class, we outsource the underlying security selection to the best asset managers in South Africa and around the world. With the maximum freedom to execute their mandate, they make their decisions and act at the right time because they know what needs to be achieved.

You benefit from diversification across both asset classes and managers, all with different management styles and market positioning. And because the SMMI mandate is sizeable, we get preferred client status.

It's possible to fly without motors.

A small team means that we act faster. We exchange information quickly. Our various backgrounds range through primary asset management, consulting, multi-management and linked product companies, so we build a bigger picture from our deeper knowledge. And we make decisions without bureaucracy or hierarchical politics.

The team has an aggregate 150 years of experience in financial markets and fund management. More telling is that we manage assets of some R90 billion, via more than 70 different funds, for over 40 000 clients.

On our global platform, SMMI advise on several Sanlam products, and on no fewer than 14 funds of UK life assurer, Merchant Investors Assurance, in several asset classes and geographic regions. SMMI is based in Cape Town and London, with fully integrated offices that share intellectual capital, proprietary tools and information to be globally competitive.

RYSZARD BIENERT | ART DIRECTOR **RYSZARD BIENERT** | DESIGNER **RYSZARD BIENERT** | CLIENT **GALERIA PIEKARY 5** | ★
PAPER/MATERIALS **COVER: 2 MM CARDBOARD, UV SPOT VARNISH, TEXT: UNCOATED OFFSET PAPER**

POLAND

★ | **BLIK** | ART DIRECTOR **TYLER BLIK** | DESIGNER **KAY TODA** | CLIENT **SGPA ARCHITECTURE + PLANNING**

USA

S DESIGN INC. | ART DIRECTOR **SARAH SEARS** | DESIGNER **MARK BOSTIAN** | CLIENT **INTERSTATE OIL AND GAS COMPACT COMMISSION** | PAPER/MATERIALS **FRENCH DUROTONE**

USA

Introduction

Before addressing the issue of how to assure the future supply of petroleum professions, it is important to put the dilemma into context.

The oil shocks of the 1970s and 1980s and the subsequent collapse in world energy prices from 1984 to 1986 resulted in a major retrenchment of the energy industry. The domestic industry alone lost more than a half million jobs in the mid-1980s. Subsequent to the price collapse that culminated in 1986, the industry has experienced substantial volatility in energy prices that has posed special challenges to maintaining a stable workforce. The price volatility continues today.

Investment in new infrastructure, refineries and other critical facilities for delivery of energy to the global economy has dropped significantly since the 1980s. This dramatic slowdown in investment has caused a large reduction in the excess delivery capacity that the industry traditionally had maintained. This loss of excess capacity is to blame, in part, for the recent spikes in prices that have occurred as the industry struggles to meet market demand in the growing global economy.

In addition, proprietary research and development (R&D) by the major operating companies were reduced dramatically as part of the austerity mindset that major operators were forced to adopt. Operators shifted from programs of highly competitive, proprietary R&D to a reliance on outside technology developed by service companies and universities. However, the funding cuts imposed by the industry during this period also affected the programs at universities and service companies and caused many of these programs to fall into ill health as well. In the same period, government-funded energy R&D also came under pressure, and dramatic reductions in federal spending made an already serious problem even worse. Federal spending continues to decline from a low level to ever lower levels. Dramatic changes in employment demographics of the energy industry then emerged. The industry hired aggressively from 1974 to 1983, and built up large staffs. Many of these people lost their jobs in the mid-1980s. In following years, those who stayed in the industry have witnessed a seemingly unending process of layoffs, reorganizations, mergers and consolidation. The "survivors," who are a large part of the current employment base of the industry, are now

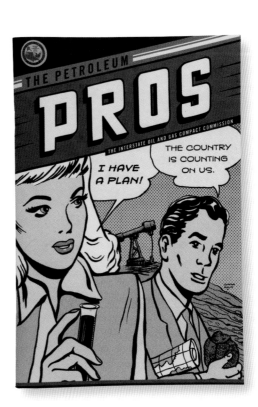

★ **HELENA SEO DESIGN** | ART DIRECTOR **HELENA SEO** | DESIGNER **HELENA SEO** | CLIENT **VIVENDI DEVELOPMENT**
PAPER/MATERIALS **STARWHITE SIRIUS SMOOTH, 130 LB. DTC, CENTURA MATTE TEXT, 100 LB.**

USA

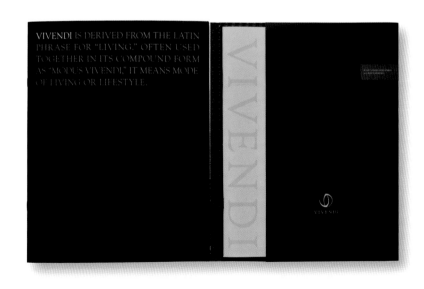

RENEE RECH DESIGN | ART DIRECTOR **RENEE RECH** | DESIGNER **RENEE RECH** | CLIENT **BANANA REPUBLIC** | ★
PAPER/MATERIALS **SMART PAPER: CARNIVAL COVER (COCO & SKY), NEENAH ENVIRONMENT TEXT, VELLUM–REICH PAPER, RIVETS, FOIL STAMPING, LEATHER CORD**

USA

BANANA REPUBLIC
DISTRICT MANAGER ONBOARDING

★ **SIMON & GOETZ DESIGN** | ART DIRECTOR **BERND VOLLMÖLLER** | DESIGNER **BERND VOLLMÖLLER**
CLIENT **SAL. OPPENHEIM JR. & CIE. KGAA** | PAPER/MATERIALS **GALAXI SUPERMAT, GALAXI KERAMIK**

Freiheit

Im Kern ist Freiheit die Abwesenheit von Zwang bei der Wahl von Handlungsalternativen. Heute wird grundsätzlich zwischen „negativer Freiheit" — bezogen auf die Pressefreiheit ist darunter beispielsweise die Möglichkeit der freien Meinungsäußerung zu verstehen – und „positiver Freiheit" unterschieden. In letzterem Fall bedeutet dies die Bereitstellung von Kommunikationsmitteln.

Wider die Zwänge

DIE IDEE DER FREIHEIT GERÄT INTELLEKTUELL IMMER MEHR IN DIE DEFENSIVE. EIN GESPRÄCH MIT
LORD RALF DAHRENDORF ZUR AKTUELLEN DEBATTE UM EINEN PHILOSOPHISCHEN BEGRIFF.

DIE PHILOSOPHIE DER FREIHEIT BEGANN EINST IN DEM Bestreben, Sklaverei und Leibeigenschaft abzuschaffen. In der Phase der Aufklärung meinte Freiheit den Ausbruch aus überkommenem Denken und die politische Überwindung vormoderner Strukturen. Ziele waren sowohl die Trennung von Staat und Kirche als auch die Einführung der Gewaltenteilung als Grundlage für Rechtsstaatlichkeit und Demokratie. Gleichzeitig wurde von nun an auch darüber gestritten, wie weit Freiheit gehen dürfe. Mit Begriffen wie Pflicht und Verantwortung wurde die Freiheitsidee ethisch eingegrenzt. Heute wird grundsätzlich zwischen negativer und positiver Freiheit unterschieden. Während unter negativer Freiheit (oder „Freiheit von") zum Beispiel eine zensurfreie Meinungsäußerung verstanden wird, bezieht sich die positive Freiheit (oder „Freiheit zu") auf die Bereitstellung von Kommunikationsmitteln, damit die Meinungsäußerung auch realisiert werden kann.

Nach der kristallklaren Definition des liberalen Soziologen Lord Ralf Dahrendorf bedeutet Freiheit im Kern die Abwesenheit von Zwang, das heißt die Fähigkeit und den Willen, zu tun und zu lassen, was man möchte. Ein Grundsatz der Freiheit lautet: Je größer die Nichteinmischung, desto größer die persönliche Freiheit. In der praktischen Umsetzung bedarf es jedoch einer Verfassung der Freiheit in Gestalt einer liberalen Ordnung, die strenggenommen eine Limitierung der reinen Freiheit darstellt. Dieser Freiheitsbegriff scheint heute durch Gerechtigkeitspostulate, ökonomische Verkürzungen und Sicherheitsdogmen in die intellektuelle Defensive geraten zu sein. Die aktuellen Bedrohungen der Freiheit

haben zugenommen. Wieviel Mut zur Verteidigung ist sie uns noch wert? Darüber unterhielt sich der Publizist Norbert Seitz mit Lord Ralf Dahrendorf.

Ausgehend von der Unterscheidung des britischen Philosophen Isaiah Berlin zwischen „positiver" und „negativer" Freiheit, wäre zu fragen, warum es aus Ihrer Sicht eine „positive" oder „soziale Freiheit" als eine Erweiterung des individuellen Handlungsspielraums durch den Staat nicht geben kann?

LORD DAHRENDORF: Das ist ein Mißbrauch. Wir sollten Dinge nicht beim falschen Namen nennen, und Freiheit ist eines und Gerechtigkeit ist ein anderes. Es gibt sehr wohl soziale Voraussetzungen einer für alle zugänglichen Freiheit. Aber man sollte es nicht Freiheit nennen. Und schon gar nicht sollte man es aufwiegen gegen andere Grundfreiheiten. Anders gesprochen: Freiheit ist Freiheit ist Freiheit, Gerechtigkeit ist Gerechtigkeit ist Gerechtigkeit.

GLOBALISIERUNG

Wie hat sich die Balance zwischen Freiheit und Gerechtigkeit durch die grenzensprengende Globalisierung verschoben?

LORD DAHRENDORF: Die neuen Entwicklungen haben natürlich enorme Freiheitsmöglichkeiten gebracht. Gleichzeitig sind neue Ungleichheiten in einem bislang nicht bekannten Ausmaß entstanden. Die unteren zehn Prozent in den USA haben beispielsweise in

---

REVOLUTION IN TÖNEN

REVOLUTION DER VERSOHNUNG?

FREE JAZZ – SCHON DIE NAMENSGEBUNG SOLLTE FÜR

Der Free-Jazz entwickelte sich in einer politischen Umbruchszeit.

Einschalten und Wohlfühlen

POPULÄRKULTUR UND HOCHKULTUR

Radio ist die Wiege der Telemoralität.

★ | **NASSAR DESIGN** | ART DIRECTOR **NELIDA NASSAR** | DESIGNER **NELIDA NASSAR** | CLIENT **HARVARD DESIGN SCHOOL**
PAPER/MATERIALS **TEXT: COUGAR SMOOTH, 80 LB., COVER: COUGAR SMOOTH, 100 LB.**

USA

Piers

[Alex Song MAUD]
[Yang Lu MUP]

The premise of this project was that the valuable water's edge could be multiplied to increase availability of housing at the waterfront. An analysis of dimensional characteristics of waterfront pier development in several major cities guided the grain and frequency of proposed new piers and density of housing for a new definition of the water's edge. The project eliminated Maine Avenue and concentrated all activity on Water Street, which was reconceived with building on both sides. A developed promenade at its present location links all the piers from the new hotel at the northern end, to the housing piers to the south. The basin defined by the hotel reaching out to the water and ferry pier at the foot of the 10th Street Mall provides a focus of public activity for the Piers development.

DIE TRANSFORMER | ART DIRECTOR/DESIGNER **MARTIN SCHONHOFF, MICHAEL THEILE**
CLIENT **BUNDESVERBAND DRUCK & MEDIEN E.V.** | PAPER/MATERIALS **FLUORESCENT COLOR, DIE CUT, HOT FOIL STAMPING**

★ **BOCCALATTE** | ART DIRECTOR **SUZANNE BOCCALATTE** | DESIGNER **SUZANNE BOCCALATTE**
CLIENT **CAMPBELLTOWN ART CENTRE** | PAPER/MATERIALS **MEGA GLOSS, OPTICS YELLOW**

AUSTRALIA

KIMIKO CHAN DESIGN | ART DIRECTOR **KIMIKO CHAN** | DESIGNER **KIMIKO CHAN** | CLIENT **ETUDE WINES** ★
PAPER/MATERIALS **MOHAWK SUPERFINE EGGSHELL COVER AND TEXT**

A MODEL FOR SUSTAINABLE VITICULTURE

*"This is the most remarkable vineyard I've ever worked with. Being
involved in a project with such a strong emphasis on protecting the
environment and natural habitat as well as on farming small
vineyards with different terroirs is very rewarding."*

— *Francis Ashton, Etude Viticulturist*

The Etude Estate Vineyards are a model for sustainable viticulture and they were carefully
designed to be just that. The vision for the Grace Benoist Ranch encompassed a long-term
concept of sustainability that included sensitivity to the environment, minimal impact on
neighbors and the community, and economic feasibility to implement and maintain.

Mindful of their roles as stewards of this special property,
the Etude team adheres strictly to sustainable agricultural
practices that enable them to farm in concert with the
surrounding environment. Native flora and naturally
occurring wetlands have been protected, and creeks are
being restored. Wildlife has been afforded safe passage-
ways through the vineyards.

KEY STEPS TAKEN TO PROTECT THE ENVIRONMENT INCLUDE:
· No oak tree removal
· Large riparian setbacks
· Protection of designated wetlands
· Protection of diverse animal and plant species around the vineyard
· Habitat corridors created to protect the abundant wildlife on the ranch

WESTERN UPLAND SLOPES OF ETUDE ESTATE VINEYARDS

NATIVE FLORA CHAMOMILE – *Matricaria recutita*
CHAMOMILE IS A MEMBER OF THE ASTER FAMILY, AND IS SOMETIMES REFERRED
TO AS MATRICARIA CHAMOMILLA AND GERMAN CHAMOMILE. AN ANNUAL, IT
GROWS FREELY EVERYWHERE AND FLOWERS IN SPRING. CHAMOMILE IS USED
FOR MEDICINAL PURPOSES, AND IS USUALLY ADMINISTERED AS A TEA.
IN THE ETUDE ESTATE VINEYARDS, THE CHAMOMILE GROWS IN BIG
COLONIES THROUGHOUT THE VINEYARD, CREATING A BLANKET OF WHITE
FLOWERS. IT'S A SHORT-LIVED BEAUTY AS IT BLOOMS AND DISAPPEARS.

FRANCIS ASHTON IN THE
ESTATE VINEYARDS

ICELAND

TIMBER DESIGN CO. INC | ART DIRECTOR **LARS LAWSON** | DESIGNER **LARS LAWSON** | ★
CLIENT **HANCOCK REGIONAL HOSPITAL** | PAPER/MATERIALS **MOHAWK–BECKETT ENHANCE**

USA

★ **SHINE ADVERTISING** | ART DIRECTOR **MICHAEL KRIEFSKI, JOHN KRULL** | DESIGNER **CHAD BOLLENBACH**
CLIENT **MADISON MALLARDS** | PAPER/MATERIALS **FINCH FINE VANILLA**

USA

★ COLD BEER ★
COMPENSATION

A Morale-Sapped Employee™, also known as an MSE, often feels under-appreciated, underpaid, and, of course, overworked (Fig. 3a). In response, many businesses prematurely resort to extreme measures to alleviate the problems at hand. These typically include: **A)** Giving an MSE a job title that indicates "*more responsibility,*" usually accomplished with the simple addition of the word "director" to an existing job title. **B)** Increasing an MSE's salary to accommodate the newly anointed "director" nomenclature. The good news? There exists a cheap and frosty alternative: beer. Cold beer. And yes, it flows free and unfettered at a Madison Mallards baseball game. With our help and expertise, that MSE in accounting will be a full-fledged BFE (Beer-Filled Employee™) by the top of the 3rd inning (Fig. 3b).

ENJOY THE BUDWEISER® SOLID ROCK ROOFTOP
(See p. 8) Employees having fun. Clients having fun. Mission accomplished. The Budweiser® Solid Rock Rooftop offers unlimited ballpark food, bottomless drinks, and a personal wait staff. For large groups, ask about renting the entire left field building, which includes the Budweiser® Solid Rock Rooftop and Outback Steakhouse Suites. ***Call 246-4277 today.***

(Fig. 3a) "My boss, Mr. Murray, is an idiot."

(Fig. 3b) "Well, hello there, Mr. Murray."

4

5

MADISON MALLARDS
ILLUSTRATED
GUIDE
To Employee
HAPPINESS & MORALE

MORALE. MOTIVATION. MALLARDS.

★ MOTIVATION ★
THROUGH HOT DOGS

Every year, thousands of businesses lose thousands of dollars due to low employee morale (Fig. 2a). We like to call it the High Cost of Low Morale Factor.™ The dilemma? How do you "fire up" a lethargic and despondent workforce without constantly threatening to fire them? Unfortunately, the answer isn't Hawaiian Shirt Friday,™ company picnic sack races, or putting together a Fun Committee.™ No, the solution is hot dogs. Good, old-fashioned American hot dogs. The kind that are plump and plentiful at every Madison Mallards baseball game. In fact, recent research indicates that workers who eat hot dogs are more productive and use fewer sick days than their non-hot-dog-eating counterparts (Fig. 2b). The bottom line: nothing puts a smile on an employee's face like a big, juicy wiener.

RESERVE THE OUTBACK STEAKHOUSE SUITES
(See p. 8) Motivate your workforce! Entertain your clients! The Outback Steakhouse Suites offer an exclusive private setting with your own personal wait staff. Enjoy ballpark food and a catered meal from the Outback Steakhouse with unlimited soda and beer. ***Call 246-4277 today.***

(Fig. 2a) "I hate my job."

(Fig. 2b) "Of course I can work this weekend!"

2

3

RIGSBY HULL | ART DIRECTOR **THOMAS HULL, LANA RIGSBY** | DESIGNER **THOMAS HULL** | CLIENT **WALTER P. MOORE**
PAPER/MATERIALS **MOHAWK SUPERFINE ULTIMATE WHITE** ★

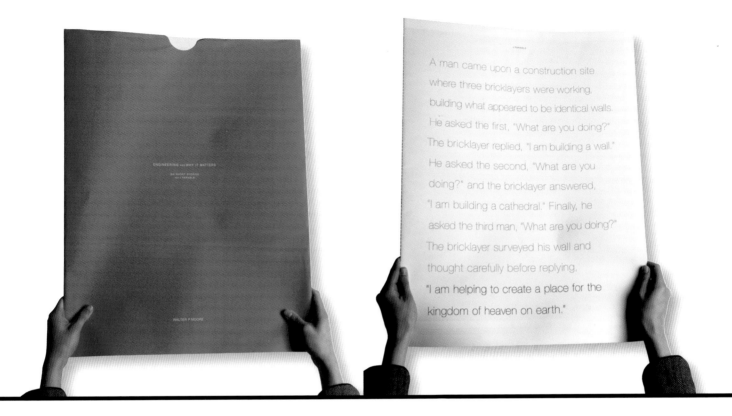

A man came upon a construction site where three bricklayers were working, building what appeared to be identical walls. He asked the first, "What are you doing?" The bricklayer replied, "I am building a wall." He asked the second, "What are you doing?" and the bricklayer answered, "I am building a cathedral." Finally, he asked the third man, "What are you doing?" The bricklayer surveyed his wall and thought carefully before replying, "I am helping to create a place for the kingdom of heaven on earth."

★ | **RIGSBY HULL** | ART DIRECTOR **THOMAS HULL** | DESIGNER **THOMAS HULL, LANA RIGSBY** | CLIENT **WALTER P. MOORE**
PAPER/MATERIALS **MOHAWK SUPERFINE ULTIMATE WHITE**

USA

NEO DESIGN | ART DIRECTOR **CRAIG HUTTON** | DESIGNER **CRAIG HUTTON** | CLIENT **PROSPERO** | ★

UNITED KINGDOM

NEO DESIGN | ART DIRECTOR **CRAIG HUTTON** | DESIGNER **CRAIG HUTTON** | CLIENT **HOWIE WHITE RECRUITMENT** | ★

★ | **VOICE ADD PTE LTD** | ART DIRECTOR **JASON LEONG, ANDROS WONG** | DESIGNER **JERRY YAU**
CLIENT **MASONRY PTE LTD** | PAPER/MATERIALS **COVER AND TEXT: EXEL BULKY**

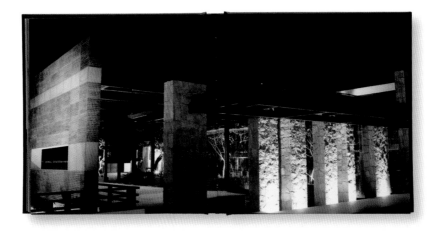

BLIK | ART DIRECTOR **TYLER BLIK** | DESIGNER **ANDREW GLENDINNING** | CLIENT **GREENWORKS STUDIO**
PAPER/MATERIALS **MOHAWK AND NEENAH ENVIRONMENT** ★

USA

★ | **SALTERBAXTER** | ART DIRECTOR **JAMES WILSON** | DESIGNER **STEWART CLARK, JENNIFER CHARON**
CLIENT **LAWRENCE GRAHAM** | PAPER/MATERIALS **MAGNO MATTE**

UNITED KINGDOM

THE CHASE | ART DIRECTOR **STEPHEN ROYLE** | DESIGNER **STEPHEN ROYLE** | ★
CLIENT **ROYAL COLLEGE OF PATHOLOGISTS** | PAPER/MATERIALS **NEENAH CLASSIC CREST AND CHIPBOARD**

USA

★ **SALTERBAXTER** | ART DIRECTOR **JAMES WILSON** | DESIGNER **CHRIS OATES, HANNAH GRIFFITHS, JENNIFER CHARON**
CLIENT **SALTERBAXTER** | PAPER/MATERIALS **THINK BRIGHT**

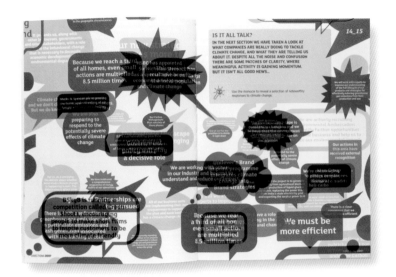

IS IT ALL TALK?

IN THE NEXT SECTION WE HAVE TAKEN A LOOK AT WHAT COMPANIES ARE REALLY DOING TO TACKLE CLIMATE CHANGE, AND WHAT THEY ARE TELLING US ABOUT IT. DESPITE ALL THE NOISE AND CONFUSION THERE ARE SOME PATCHES OF CLARITY, WHERE MEANINGFUL ACTIVITY IS GAINING MOMENTUM. BUT IT ISN'T ALL GOOD NEWS...

Use the mouse to reveal a selection of noteworthy responses to climate change.

Tackling climate change – why us?

Al Gore's film title 'An Inconvenient Truth' could not have summed up the situation better. It is only human nature to resist what is not seen as convenient.

Rt. Hon. John Gummer
Chairman of Sancroft International and Chairman of the Quality of Life Policy

no **PAIN** no **gain**

Fighting
climate change
– as well as other challenges to sustainable business

Julia Cleverdon
Chief Executive of Business in the Community

With corporate attention focused on climate change, some are asking whether companies should return to the 'green' roots of corporate responsibility. Julia Cleverdon argues that companies taking this approach are missing the point.

The role of business in tackling climate change has been thrust onto centre stage over the past 12 months. Sir Nicholas Stern's Review of the Economics of Climate Change highlighted the need for businesses to reduce their carbon dioxide emissions to avoid severe economic consequences, and the UN's Intergovernmental Panel on Climate Change (IPCC) emphasised the short time window for action, with emissions needing to peak and decline within the next 20 years.

This has not gone unnoticed by the corporate world. Out of the 1,000 business leaders that attended this year's Prince of Wales's May Day Business Summit on Climate Change, nearly two thirds saw climate change as a risk for their business. What is encouraging, however, is that 90% also saw the opportunities it offered, whether through cost savings, new market opportunities or as a driver to engage and retain employees' trust.

It is those companies that truly understand those opportunities that are making a real difference. Take for example BSkyB, winner of the Man Group International Climate Change Award 2007. It recognised the consumer desire for affordable green products and introduced

the world's first set-top box with an automatic standby facility. It has also now engaged employees in eco-schools. BT has taken a different angle, working closely with its suppliers to produce products that have a lower carbon footprint than their predecessors, so emissions savings can be passed on to its customers.

These companies are successfully combining the reduction of their environmental footprint with business benefits, and continuing to create wealth for the UK. And they should be commended and used to inspire other companies, some of whom are only just beginning their climate change journey.

But to see corporate responsibility just through the lens of climate change would be to miss the rich mix of issues on which business has been making an impact.

Taking a broader approach
When Business in the Community was formed 25 years ago in the wake of race riots and social unrest in the UK, the purpose of the group of leading businesses was to work collaboratively to tackle the key social issues of the day. Since

UNITED KINGDOM

★ **SALTERBAXTER** | ART DIRECTOR **JAMES WILSON** | DESIGNER **HANNAH GRIFFITHS** | CLIENT **SALTERBAXTER**
PAPER/MATERIALS **THINK4 BRIGHT**

UNITED KINGDOM

EBD | ART DIRECTOR **ELLEN BRUSS** | DESIGNER **GORDON CHISLETT** | CLIENT **WYNKOOP RESIDENCES** ★
PAPER/MATERIALS **NEENAH CLASSIC CREST AND CHIPBOARD**

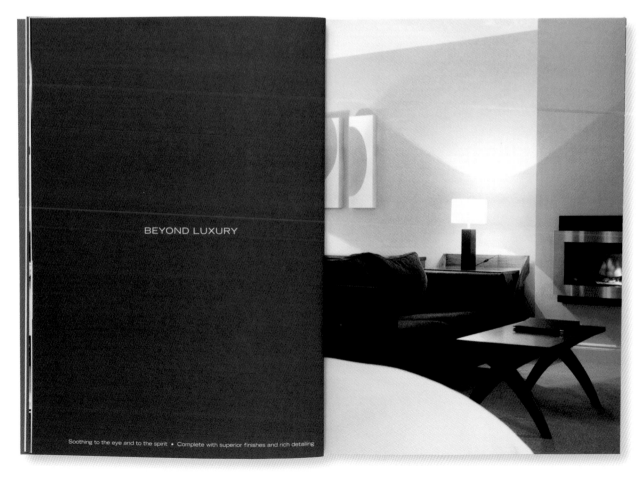

BEYOND LUXURY

Soothing to the eye and to the spirit • Complete with superior finishes and rich detailing

USA

★

IN THIS SECTION

PRODUCT
AND
SERVICE

★ | **URBANINFLUENCE** | ART DIRECTOR **MIKE MATES, PETE WRIGHT** | DESIGNER **MIKE MATES, BRAD SHERMAN**
CLIENT **HILTON HOTELS**

USA

USA

YOU'RE INVITED

to Twenty Years
of the Queen

AN EXCLUSIVE V.I.P.
ANNIVERSARY CELEBRATION

Thursday, May 24th 5-7pm

THE QUEEN WANTS TO THANK SEATTLE FOR 20 GREAT YEARS!

JOIN US FOR A SPECIAL EVENING OF THANKS AND A CHANCE TO TRY A FEW OF
OUR SIGNATURE DISHES, AS WELL AS SOME NEW FAVORITES. WE'LL BE POURING
WINES FROM OUR ANNIVERSARY SELECTION — 20 GREAT WINES PRICED UNDER
$20 — AS WELL AS KICKING OFF OUR THREE COURSE DINNER MENU FOR $20 PER
PERSON. WE HOPE YOU'LL JOIN US FOR THE CELEBRATION.

THE FRESHLY RENOVATED QUEEN CITY GRILL:
2201 FIRST AVENUE, SEATTLE, WA 98121

QUEEN CITY
GRILL

R.S.V.P.

R.S.V.P. FOR THIS EVENT AT WWW.QUEENCITYGRILL.COM/20 BY MAY 22ND
or
FILL OUT THIS TICKET AND MAIL TO: DUO, 3609 1ST AVE. NW, SEATTLE, WA 98107

NAME:

PHONE:

EMAIL:

GUEST?   YES   NO

★ **RETHINK** | CREATIVE DIRECTOR **IAN GRAIS / CHRIS STAPLES** | DESIGNER **LISA NAKAMURA** | CLIENT **BARE**
PAPER/MATERIALS **COVER: 80 LB. PACESETTER MATTE COVER TEXT: 70 LB. PACESETTER TEXT WHITE**

CANADA

KARACTERS DESIGN GROUP | ART DIRECTOR **MARIA KENNEDY** | DESIGNER **TIM HOFFPAUIR** | CLIENT **VANOC** | ★
PAPER/MATERIALS **MOHAWK OPTIONS, REICH PAPER CT. SOFT**

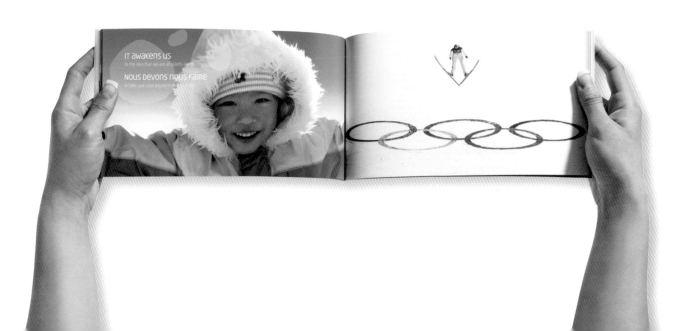

★ | **WALTERWAKEFIELD** | ART DIRECTOR **JAIMY WALTER** | DESIGNER **PHOEBE BESLEY, MARIANNE MALAFOSSE, JAIMY WALTER**
CLIENT **SPICERS PAPER** | PAPER/MATERIALS **MONZA RECYCLED (VARIOUS) 130–400 GSM**

AUSTRALIA

High Definition

GIMME
GIMME
GIMME

Madonna's single *Gimme Up* features a
sample of *Abba's Gimme Gimme Gimme
(A Man After Midnight)*. The sample is a
huge win for Madonna who became one
of the rare artists to be endorsed by *Abba*
to use one of their works as a sample.

Previously only *Cilla Ruspoli* were granted
this honor by *Abba* when they used a
sample from *Get Name of the Game* in their
1996 track *Rumble in the Jungle*. *Nirvana*
and *Aqua* from *Abba* broke their strict
"no sample" rule on this occasion.

Gimme Up was the first single from the
album *Confessions on a Dance Floor*.

monza
recycled

Mixed Sources

The album *Living my Life* begins with *My
Jamaican Guy*, a reggae influenced mid-
tempo track. *Grace Jones* wrote the song
in Jamaican patois in parts, giving the
track a quirky feel.

If you listen to it, you realise that *L L Cool J*
sampled parts of this track in his song
Doin' it. The album spawned three singles,
My Jamaican Guy, *Apple to the Bottle* and
Everybody Holds Still.

monza
recycled

Mixed Sources

Clarity

★ **DESIGN ARMY** | ART DIRECTOR **PUM LEFEBURE, JAKE LEFEBURE** | DESIGNER **TAYLOR BUCKHOLZ**
CLIENT **GOLDEN TRIANGLE BUSINESS IMPROVEMENT DISTRICT** | PAPER/MATERIALS **COUGAR, DIE CUT, GOLD FOIL STAMPING**

GOLDEN OPPORTUNITY

MEET YOUR NEIGHBORS

Live amongst the most stylish, glamorous and delicious neighbors in all of DC. A bustling, urban area filled with upscale names like The Hay Adams Hotel, Equinox Restaurant and BLT Steak, the Golden Triangle offers an ideal mix of big businesses, cool shops, fabulous restaurants and world-renowned salons. Not to mention, upscale hotels that average around $400/night. Just think, you could live next door to a trendy store known as Thomas Pink or one that's more classic like Brooks Brothers. Maybe you'd rather be closer to the Mayflower or one of the countless amazing restaurants. With an incredible $735 per square foot in sales among apparel retailers, this is your golden opportunity to be a part of one of the smartest neighborhoods in the city.

GOLDEN TRIANGLE

Imagine a place in the heart of Washington DC filled with highly successful urban professionals looking for convenient shopping. A place just steps away from the White House, K Street and upscale hotels where the most discriminating visitors stay. A luxurious place where DC powerbrokers and travelers alike can stroll down a bustling, tree-lined street and find *Burberry* on their left, *Thomas Pink* on their right and a gem called the *Tiny Jewel Box* tucked in between. And when they've had their fill of high fashion, can stop for a delectable bite to eat at *The Palm* followed by a hair appointment at a trendy salon. Imagine a place that includes many major Metro stops and wealthy residential neighborhoods where a concert in the park can be heard in the summertime. A place like no other. **Welcome to the Golden Triangle.**

Whether for a business breakfast, a lunch meeting or post-work cocktails, the Golden Triangle is the ideal setting to name everything from a quick bite to a five-star meal at one of the most fabulous and fashionable restaurants in Washington DC.

USA

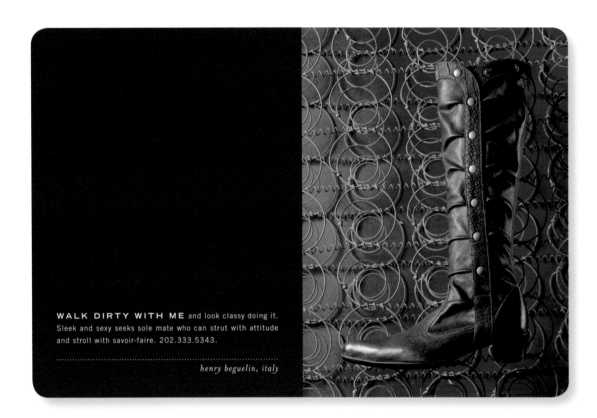

WALK DIRTY WITH ME and look classy doing it.
Sleek and sexy seeks sole mate who can strut with attitude
and stroll with savoir-faire. 202.333.5343.

henry beguelin, italy

LITTLE BLACK BOOK
fall/winter 2004

relish

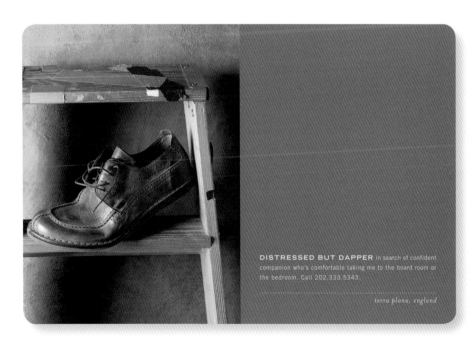

DISTRESSED BUT DAPPER in search of confident
companion who's comfortable taking me to the board room or
the bedroom. Call 202.333.5343.

terra plana, england

★ **WOW BRANDING** | DESIGNER **WILL JOHNSON, PERRY CHUA, JEFF SCHRAMM**
CLIENT **AVIVA SPORTS**

WILLOUGHBY DESIGN GROUP | ART DIRECTOR **ANN WILLOUGHBY, ZACK SHUBKAGEL** | DESIGNER **ZACK SHUBKAGEL**
CLIENT **SOUTHERN GRAPHICS COUNCIL**

USA

★ **WILLOUGHBY DESIGN GROUP** | ART DIRECTOR **ANN WILLOUGHBY, NICOLE SATTERWHITE, DEB TAGTALIANIDIS**
DESIGNER **NICOLE SATTERWHITE, RYAN JONES, JESSICA MCENTIRE** | CLIENT **MOHAWK FINE PAPERS**
PAPER/MATERIALS **STRATHMORE WRITING AND SCRIPT**

USA

WILLOUGHBY DESIGN GROUP | ART DIRECTOR **ANN WILLOUGHBY, ANNE SIMMONS**
DESIGNER **NATE HARDIN** | CLIENT **LINKS FITNESS**

★

USA

★ **THERE VISUAL COMMUNICATION DESIGN** | ART DIRECTOR **PAUL TABOURE** | DESIGNER **SIMON HANCOCK**
CLIENT **ORIENT EXPRESS HOTELS** | PAPER/MATERIALS **PREMIUM STOCK, MATTE CELLO, UV VARNISH, AND FOIL STAMPING**

AUSTRALIA

ULHAS MOSES DESIGN STUDIO | ART DIRECTOR **ULHAS MOSES** | DESIGNER **ULHAS MOSES** | CLIENT **BRITISH COUNCIL**
PAPER/MATERIALS **GRUPPO NATURAL EVOLUTION IVORY**

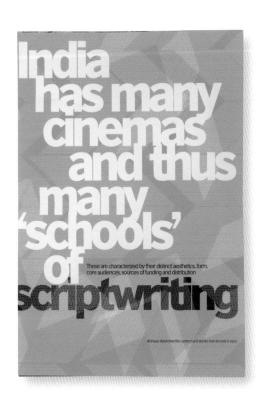

★ **ULHAS MOSES DESIGN STUDIO** | ART DIRECTOR **ULHAS MOSES** | DESIGNER **ULHAS MOSES** | CLIENT **BRITISH COUNCIL**
PAPER/MATERIALS **GRUPPO NATURAL EVOLUTION IVORY**

INDIA

ULHAS MOSES DESIGN STUDIO | ART DIRECTOR **ULHAS MOSES** | DESIGNER **ULHAS MOSES** | CLIENT **UNLTD, UK** ★
PAPER/MATERIALS **MAP LITHO**

INDIA

★ **SPRING ADVERTISING + DESIGN** | ART DIRECTOR **JAMES FILBRY, ROB SCHLYECHER** | DESIGNER **PERRY CHUA**
CLIENT **MAVERICK REAL ESTATE**

CANADA

CAMPBELL FISHER DESIGN | ART DIRECTOR **GREG FISHER** | DESIGNER **GG LEMERE** | CLIENT **MARICOPA PARTNERSHIP FOR ARTS AND CULTURE** | PAPER/MATERIALS **DOMTAR SOLUTIONS CARRERA WHITE 65 LB. COVER** | ★

USA

★ **GDC—GUGLIELMINO DESIGN CO.** | ART DIRECTOR **SID GUGLIELMINO** | DESIGNER **CHRIS DIXON**
CLIENT **ARTWORKERS ALLIANCE** | PAPER/MATERIALS **SOVEREIGN MATTE ART AND SOVEREIGN OFFSET**

AUSTRALIA

"If it looks like a lolly, I like it"

Liana Kabel

Liana Kabel has a love affair with all things plastic. The plastic objects she uses as material are rich in their associations with the 1950s housewife ideal and 'proper' feminine activities. However in Kabel's hands domesticity is thwarted and once functional objects are now loved not for their efficiency but for their vibrant colour and formal possibilities. Measuring tapes become flowers, knitting needles are transformed into bangles and Tupperware is melted to form abstract paintings to be worn as earrings or necklaces. Kabel's pieces encourage our attention to shift between the form and previous functions of these objects. The formal properties of colour, shape and line are as equally important as nostalgic qualities and domestic heritage, and this dualism allows Kabel's work to function on both aesthetic and personal levels.

By employing recycled objects from the domestic sphere, Kabel's jewellery speaks of times gone by and can evoke nostalgia for past moments that have been brought to life again through the encounter with a familiar object. As such, Kabel's works highlight the role second-hand objects can play as repositories of nostalgia, both real and created. Most of us are familiar with nostalgia as a feeling of longing and affective experience triggered by personal memories of the past. However, nostalgia can also be attached to objects and moments in time not experienced first-hand. In the latter, nostalgia is embodied in a stylised aesthetic that invokes socially constructed ideas of the past. These two concepts of nostalgia are conflated in Kabel's practice through the artist's use of recycled homewares which maintain connections to lived, everyday experience for many viewers, while simultaneously functioning on the level of retro, as fantastic plastic that embodies a culturally taught code of nostalgia.

Liana Kabel

Liana Kabel was born in Sydney and is currently based in Brisbane, Australia. Since moving location Liana's artistic practice has seen a focus on the design and handcrafted production of contemporary jewellery.

Liana's background is broad ranging having also had experience in ceramics, photography, painting, fibre arts, costume design and the performing arts. Liana has completed a Bachelor of Arts from the University of New South Wales majoring in English and Theatre Studies.

Working as a full time artist, she divides her time between her home studio and her studio at Museum of Brisbane Workspace in City Hall.

1 **Knitted rings** 2007
Knitting needles
Courtesy of the artist

2 **Pastry flower earrings** 2006
Plastic, rubber and sterling silver
Courtesy of the artist

3 **Tupperware Necklace** 2006
Tupperware and sterling silver
Courtesy of the artist
Photo: Tim Nemeth
Courtesy the Museum of Brisbane

60

BRANDEX ADVERTISING, BRANDING + DESIGN | ART DIRECTOR **TIM KELLY** | DESIGNER **KATE SIDI** | ★
CLIENT **OPPENHEIMER** | PAPER/MATERIALS **MOHAWK SUPERFINE SMOOTH**

★ | **BRANDEX ADVERTISING, BRANDING + DESIGN** | ART DIRECTOR **TIM KELLY** | DESIGNER **TIM KELLY**
 | CLIENT **OPPENHEIMER** | PAPER/MATERIALS **MOHAWK SUPERFINE SMOOTH**

BRANDEX ADVERTISING, BRANDING + DESIGN | ART DIRECTOR **TIM KELLY** | DESIGNER **KATE SIDI** | ★
CLIENT **ZESPRI KIWIFRUIT INTERNATIONAL** | PAPER/MATERIALS **MOHAWK SUPERFINE EGGSHELL**

★ **BURTON SNOWBOARDS/SYNDICATE** | ART DIRECTOR **TOBY GRUBB** | DESIGNER **CRISTIN DENIGHT** | CLIENT **BURTON**

USA

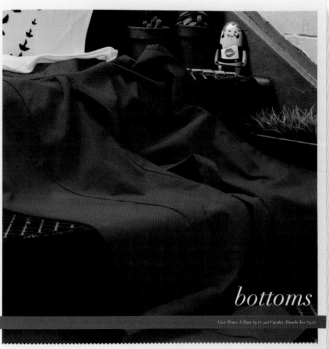

bottoms

BURTON SNOWBOARDS/SYNDICATE | ART DIRECTOR **RICH CURREN** | DESIGNER **RICH CURREN, MIKE WOOD**
CLIENT **BURTON**

★ **BURTON SNOWBOARDS/SYNDICATE** | ART DIRECTOR **TOBY GRUBB** | DESIGNER **ADAM WEISS, DOUG CLARK, CRISTIN DENIGHT**
CLIENT **BURTON**

USA

BURTON/SYNDICATE | ART DIRECTOR **ADAM WEISS** | DESIGNER **ADAM WEISS** | CLIENT **BURTON** | ★

★ | **BURTON/SYNDICATE** | ART DIRECTOR **ALEX LOWE** | DESIGNER **ADAM WEISS** | CLIENT **BURTON**

USA

USA

★ | **BURTON/SYNDICATE** | ART DIRECTOR **ALEX LOWE** | DESIGNER **ADAM WEISS** | CLIENT **BURTON**

★ **BURTON/SYNDICATE** | ART DIRECTOR **ALEX LOWE** | DESIGNER **ADAM WEISS** | CLIENT **BURTON**

USA

CREATIVE SPARK | ART DIRECTOR **NEIL MARRA** | DESIGNER **ANDY MALLALIEU** | CLIENT **POLICE SUNGLASSES** | ★
PAPER/MATERIALS **COVER: 400 GSM UNCOATED (BLOCK FOIL), LEAVES: 200 GSM GLOSS**

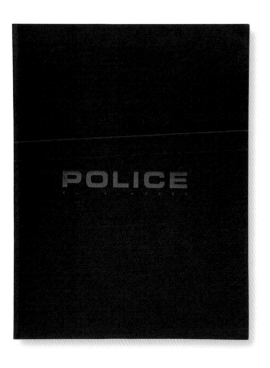

★ **DECKER DESIGN** | ART DIRECTOR **LYNDA DECKER** | DESIGNER **VIRGINIA TEVERE** | CLIENT **VISPERA**
PAPER/MATERIALS **NINA CLASSIC CREST**

USA

DESIGN RANCH | ART DIRECTOR/DESIGNER **MICHELLE SONDEREGGER, INGRED SIDIE** | CLIENT **BUCKLE** ★
PAPER/MATERIALS **CARDBOARD COVER WITH TAPE BINDING**

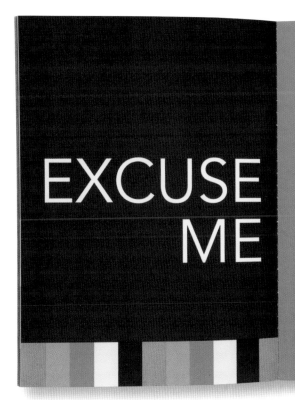

I was walking to school. Yeah. And I was jotting something in my notebook while I walked. See? Yeah. It was...extra credit. Yeah, that's it. Extra credit. And I tripped. See? And my pencil flew out of my hand. Yeah. Way into the air. Like a little rocket. Yeah, that's it. A regular Sputnik. And when it landed, it was going so fast, it buried itself in the ground. See? And it hit oil. Yeah, that's it. Oil. And there was oil everywhere. An oil spill. See? And I had to clean the oil spill. Yeah. So I grabbed the first thing I could. See? And that was my homework. Yeah, that's it. I used my homework to clean the oil spill. See? So that's why I don't have it.

★ **DESIGN RANCH** | ART DIRECTOR **MICHELLE SONDEREGGER, INGRED SIDIE** | DESIGNER **TAD CARPENTER, RACHEL KARACA, MICHELLE SONDEREGGER, INGRED SIDIE** | CLIENT **BUCKLE/LEE** | PAPER/MATERIALS **BOUND BOOK**

Jean is back. Dick is happy.

24 | 101Z | Limited Edition | 394-1441 | Real Dry

For more information or product samples contact
Angela Sciara 816.512.9160 or Jennifer Johnson 913.789.0705.

Jane considers a performance art piece involving Jean.

Jean likes performance art. Jean thinks performance art is tops.

16

17

This is Jean.

This is Jane.

2

3

This is Jean.

This is Dick.

2

3

★ **DESIGN RANCH** | ART DIRECTOR **MICHELLE SONDEREGGER, INGRED SIDIE** | DESIGNER **BRYNN JOHNSON**
CLIENT **LEE** | PAPER/MATERIALS **HARD BOUND, ACCORDION-FOLD BOOK**

USA

DESIGN RANCH | ART DIRECTOR **MICHELLE SONDEREGGER, INGRED SIDIE**
DESIGNER **TAD CARPENTER, BRYNN JOHNSON** | CLIENT **LEE**   ★

★ **HELENA SEO DESIGN** | ART DIRECTOR **HELENA SEO** | DESIGNER **HELENA SEO** | CLIENT **INEKE, LLC**
PAPER/MATERIALS **COVER: NEENAH ULTRA UV II, 28 LB., TEXT: MOHAWK SUPERFINE 100 LB.**

DESIGN RANCH | ART DIRECTOR **MICHELLE SONDEREGGER, INGRED SIDIE** | DESIGNER **BRYNN JOHNSON**
CLIENT **LEE** | PAPER/MATERIALS **ACCORDION-FOLD BOOK**

★

USA

★ **DESIGN RANCH** | ART DIRECTOR **MICHELLE SONDEREGGER, INGRED SIDIE** | DESIGNER **TAD CARPENTER**
CLIENT **RAETA ESTATES** | PAPER/MATERIALS **LETTERPRESSED CARDBOARD AND FRENCH PAPER**

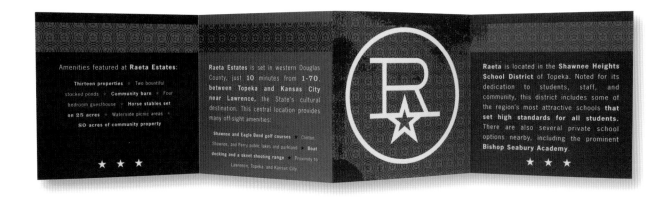

Amenities featured at **Raeta Estates**:

Thirteen properties ★ Two bountiful stocked ponds ★ **Community barn** ★ Four bedroom guesthouse ★ **Horse stables set on 25 acres** ★ Waterside picnic areas ★ **80 acres of community property**

Shawnee and Eagle Bend golf courses ★ Clinton, Shawnee, and Perry public lakes and parkland ★ **Boat docking and a skeet shooting range** ★ Proximity to Lawrence, Topeka, and Kansas City

★ ★ ★

Raeta Estates is set in western Douglas County, just **10** minutes from **I-70**, between Topeka and Kansas City near Lawrence, the State's cultural destination. This central location provides many off-sight amenities:

Raeta is located in the **Shawnee Heights School District** of Topeka. Noted for its dedication to students, staff, and community, this district includes some of the region's most attractive schools **that set high standards for all students.** There are also several private school options nearby, including the prominent **Bishop Seabury Academy.**

★ ★ ★

DESIGN RANCH | ART DIRECTOR **MICHELLE SONDEREGGER, INGRED SIDIE** | DESIGNER **MICHELLE MARTYNOWICZ, TAD CARPENTER**
CLIENT **BUCKLE** | PAPER/MATERIALS **NEWSPRINT**

★

USA

CANADA

BONBON LONDON | ART DIRECTOR **MARK HARPER, SASHA CASTLING** | DESIGNER **MARK HARPER**
CLIENT **DANIEL COBB** | PAPER/MATERIALS **NATURALIS SMOOTH RECYCLED 160 GSM AND BEDROCK**

UNITED KINGDOM

carmarthen place

★ **DEI CREATIVE** | ART DIRECTOR **SARA GREEN, SHANNON PALMER** | DESIGNER **NOAH BELL**
CLIENT **EK REAL ESTATE + TRACE LOFTS, LLC.** | PAPER/MATERIALS **MOHAWK OPTIONS, THREAD**

USA

THE O GROUP | ART DIRECTOR **JASON B. COHEN, KARIN SATROM** | DESIGNER **MARITES ALGONES, TANYA POPADICS, ALEX AMMAR**
CLIENT **MÖET HENNESSY USA** | PAPER/MATERIALS **UTOPIA U1X SILK 80 LB. COVER, GOLD FOIL EMBOSSED STICKER**

HENNESSY ELLIPSE

Hennessy Ellipse is the most exclusive cognac representing seven generations of
The House of Hennessy. Sold in hand-crafted decanters designed by Thomas Bastide,
only 200 individually numbered bottles are imported annually.

BLEND
7 eaux-de-vie selected
by 7 generations of
Hennessy Master Blenders

AROMA
Crystallized fruits, wild roses,
rancio of well-aged cognac

TASTE
Perfect combination of age
and elegance, fine blend of
subtle qualities

SERVING SUGGESTION
Neat in a crystal glass

HENNESSY ELLIPSE
RICHARD HENNESSY
PARADIS EXTRA
HENNESSY X.O
PRIVILÈGE V.S.O.P
HENNESSY V.S

HENNESSY V.S WORLD COCKTAILS

HENNESSY NEW YORK
Pour 2 oz. of Hennessy V.S
over 5 ice cubes into a snifter
or Collins glass. Fill with 6 oz.
of cola.

HENNESSY HAVANA
Muddle 10 mint sprigs and
1/2 oz. of simple syrup in
a tall glass. Add 2 oz. of
Hennessy V.S and 1 oz. of
fresh lime juice. Fill with ice
and a splash of club soda.

HENNESSY SHANGHAI
Pour 2 oz. of Hennessy V.S
over 6 ice cubes into a snifter
or Collins glass. Add a dash
of bitters, fill with 6 oz. of
ginger ale and stir.

HENNESSY PARIS
Mix in a shaker over ice: 2 oz.
Hennessy V.S, 1 oz. triple sec,
and 1 oz. sour mix. Serve in a
chilled sugar-rimmed snifter or
martini glass.

★ **THE O GROUP** | ART DIRECTOR **JASON B. COHEN, J. KENNETH ROTHERMICH** | DESIGNER **J. KENNETH ROTHERMICH**
CLIENT **NORTH DEVELOPMENT GROUP** | PAPER/MATERIALS **MOHAWK ULTRAWHITE SMOOTH 100 LB. COVER, 100 LB.**
TEXT AND 80 LB. TEXT

Number 20 Bayard will forever top out as the tallest building on either side of McCarren Park. Because new zoning rules say no one can build taller, the Brooklyn-to-Manhattan views from each apartment and the towering rooftop will always be preserved.

18
FLOORS
UP

★ | **50,000 FEET INC.** | ART DIRECTOR **TRACY WEST** | DESIGNER **TRACY WEST, JOHNNY MEI**
CLIENT **MINI/BMW OF NORTH AMERICA, LLC.** | PAPER/MATERIALS **SAPPI LUSTRO GLOSS 100 LB. COVER**

USA

RALLY INTERNATIONAL ICON

MINI MOTORINGGEAR FALL / WINTER 2007

Most stories follow a time-honored formula: beginning, middle and end. But in the world of MINI, things work a little differently. For instance, you might start out in one direction only to veer off in another. Or discover that an end is really a beginning in disguise. In that spirit, we're proud to present a trio of new collections from MINI MotoringGear, engineered for spinning on- and off-road tales in inimitable MINI style. **RALLY COLLECTION** A race-inspired throwback to a time when MINI reigned supreme in Monte Carlo and the world was put on notice. **INTERNATIONAL COLLECTION** Eye-grabbing designs drawn from an ever-growing MINI nation that stretches across countries and continents alike. **ICON COLLECTION** Classic colors and timeless lines converge in a look that's pure, unadulterated MINI. Outfitted with this introduction, you're ready to write your own chapter in motoring history. We trust that, as with any great road, it'll have more than enough twists and turns to keep things interesting.

EVERY STORY HAS TO START SOMEWHERE.

50,000 FEET INC. | ART DIRECTOR **TRACY WEST** | DESIGNER **JOHNNY MEI, TRACY WEST** ★
CLIENT **MINI/BMW OF NORTH AMERICA, LLC.** | PAPER/MATERIALS **SAPPI OPUS**

USA

★ | **50,000 FEET INC.** | ART DIRECTOR **MICHAEL PETERSEN** | DESIGNER **MICHAEL PETERSEN** | CLIENT **TERLATO WINES**
PAPER/MATERIALS **MOHAWK SUPERFINE ULTRAWHITE**

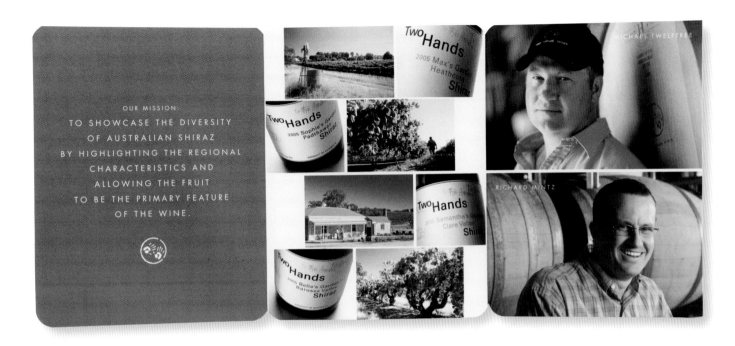

OUR MISSION:
TO SHOWCASE THE DIVERSITY
OF AUSTRALIAN SHIRAZ
BY HIGHLIGHTING THE REGIONAL
CHARACTERISTICS AND
ALLOWING THE FRUIT
TO BE THE PRIMARY FEATURE
OF THE WINE.

MICHAEL TWELFTREE

RICHARD MINTZ

MAX'S GARDEN ~ HEATHCOTE

Located 75 miles north of Melbourne in Central Victoria, the climate and soils are strongly influenced by the Mount Camel Range, which provides a natural tunneling for the prevailing cool south to southeast winds. The secret here is the oldest soil in Australia, deep red Cambrian pulverized rock that is 500 million years old. Heathcote produces world-class Shiraz with distinctive character, depth and richness.

TASTING NOTES

HARRY & EDWARD'S GARDEN ~ LANGHORNE CREEK

Situated 30 miles south of Adelaide, it is centered on the floodplains of the Bremer River. Many times the river floods during Spring providing an efficient and old-fashioned form of irrigation. The climate is shaped by the onshore southerly winds blowing from the ocean across Lake Alexandrina, reducing daytime temperature fluctuations. Langhorne Creek Shiraz is typically rich and concentrated with a famous soft mellow quality.

TASTING NOTES

CLARE VALLEY

Located 70 miles north of Adelaide, it has a moderate continental climate. Altitude, position and exposure lead to considerable variations in individual site climate. Cool enough in parts to produce pristine Riesling, but warm enough to fully ripen Shiraz, Clare Valley is capable of producing concentrated Shiraz with elegant restraint.

TASTING NOTES

LILY'S GARDEN ~ McLAREN VALE

Located 25 miles south of Adelaide bordered by the Gulf of St. Vincent to the west, Sellicks Hills Range to the south and Adelaide Hills to the east. The gulf creates cooling sea breezes that sweep across the vineyards. McLaren Vale produces Shiraz with dark plum and mulberry fruit profiles, with distinct dark chocolate tones and soft, supple tannins.

TASTING NOTES

BELLA'S GARDEN ~ BAROSSA VALLEY

Located 45 miles northeast of Adelaide, the Barossa Valley is the principle region from which Two Hands sources 60% of its fruit. The Mediterranean climate is perfect for producing the full-bodied Shiraz for which the Barossa Valley is renowned.

TASTING NOTES

SOPHIE'S GARDEN ~ PADTHAWAY

Part of the greater Limestone Coast region, Padthaway is located in the lower southeast of the state of South Australia. Slightly cooler than the regions to its north, it has a Mediterranean climate with a maritime influence due to the absence of mountains. The soil here is the famous terra rossa over limestone. Shiraz from Padthaway is full-bodied and dense with dark-berried fruit displaying intense spicy overtones.

TASTING NOTES

USA

★ | **50,000 FEET INC.** | ART DIRECTOR **KEN FOX, TRACY WEST** | DESIGNER **TRACY WEST, ADAM DINES**
CLIENT **TERLATO WINES** | PAPER/MATERIALS **MOHAWK SUPERFINE ULTRAWHITE, SIERRA BOOK CLOTH**

★ **50,000 FEET INC.** | ART DIRECTOR **KEN FOX, JIM MISENER** | DESIGNER **TRACY WEST** | CLIENT **TERLATO WINES**
PAPER/MATERIALS **MOHAWK SUPERFINE ULTRAWHITE**

USA

NOTHING: SOMETHING: NY | ART DIRECTOR **KEVIN LANDWEHR** | DESIGNER **KEVIN LANDWEHR, DEVIN BECKER, SHOKO TSUJI**
CLIENT **CLOAK & DAGGER** | PAPER/MATERIALS **FRENCH PAPER**

★ **NOTHING: SOMETHING: NY** | ART DIRECTOR **KEVIN LANDWEHR** | DESIGNER **KEVIN LANDWEHR, DEVIN BECKER, KEVIN DEVINE**
CLIENT **EDUN-ROGAN, ALI HEWSON, BONO** | PAPER/MATERIALS **PLIKE, KROMEKOTE, LASER CUTTING AND FOIL STAMPING**

USA

NOTHING: SOMETHING: NY | ART DIRECTOR **KEVIN LANDWEHR** | DESIGNER **KEVIN LANDWEHR, DEVIN BECKER**
CLIENT **MADE HER THINK/MEREDITH KAHN**

★

USA

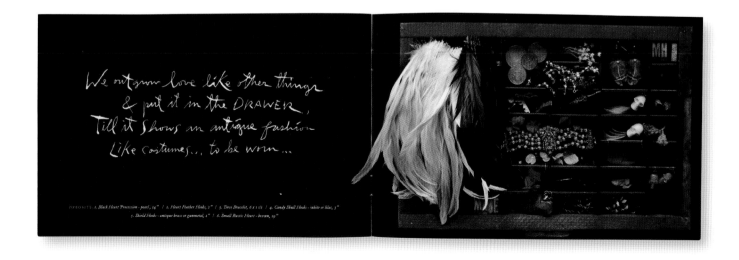

★ **NOTHING: SOMETHING: NY** | ART DIRECTOR **KEVIN LANDWEHR** | DESIGNER **KEVIN LANDWEHR, DEVIN BECKER**
CLIENT MADE HER THINK/MEREDITH KAHN

KORN DESIGN | ART DIRECTOR **DENISE KORN** | DESIGNER **MELISSA WEHRMAN**
CLIENT **LXR LUXURY RESORTS/THE LONDON NYC HOTEL** | PAPER/MATERIALS **MOHAWK SUPERFINE, MOHAWK NAVAJO**

USA

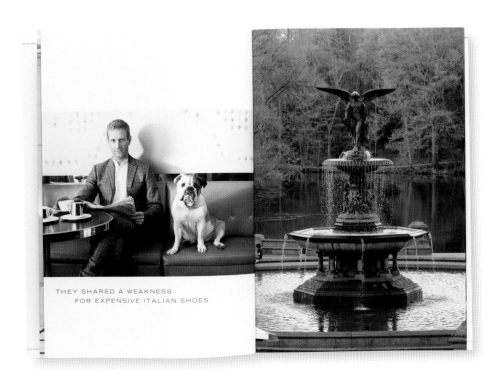

THEY SHARED A WEAKNESS
FOR EXPENSIVE ITALIAN SHOES

SHE WAS ALWAYS
FASHIONABLY LATE

★ **KORN DESIGN** | ART DIRECTOR **DENISE KORN** | DESIGNER **MELISSA WEHRMAN**
CLIENT **LXR LUXURY RESORTS/THE LONDON NYC HOTEL** | PAPER/MATERIALS **MOHAWK SUPERFINE, MOHAWK NAVAJO**

USA

PROPELLER | ART DIRECTOR **TODD FRIEDMAN, BRIAN EICKHOFF** | DESIGNER **BRIAN EICKHOFF**
CLIENT **MAX STRANG ARCHITECTURE** | PAPER/MATERIALS **SHELL: STRATHMORE PREMIUM OPAQUE WHITE SMOOTH
160 LB. COVER, INSERTS: STRATHMORE PREMIUM OPAQUE WHITE SMOOTH 130 LB. COVER**

★

USA

★ **DESIGN RANCH** │ ART DIRECTOR **MICHELLE SONDEREGGER, INGRED SIDIE** │ DESIGNER **TAD CARPENTER, RACHEL KARACA**
CLIENT **LEE** │ PAPER/MATERIALS **VELLUM AND NEWSPRINT, FRENCH FOLDED AND INDUSTRIAL STAPLED**

USA

LISKA + ASSOCIATES | ART DIRECTOR **STEVE LISKA** | DESIGNER **VANESSA REU, STEVE LISKA**
CLIENT **CRANE & CO.** | PAPER/MATERIALS **CRANE'S CREST, 32 LB.**

★

USA

★ **DESIGNBOLAGET** | ART DIRECTOR **CLAUS DUE** | DESIGNER **CLAUS DUE** | CLIENT **STELLA NOVA**
PAPER/MATERIALS **SLEEVE IN MIRRORBOARD**

DENMARK

DENMARK

★ **DESIGNBOLAGET** | ART DIRECTOR **CLAUS DUE** | DESIGNER **EMIL GAMMELGAARD, HENRIETTE KRUSE**
CLIENT **WONHUNDRED** | PAPER/MATERIALS **4 DIFFERENT PAPER QUALITIES**

WON HUNDRED

www.wonhundred.com

ARE WE THE SAME, WITH
DIFFERENCES?
OR DIFFERENT
WITH SIMILARITIES?
18-19

- Ten -

★ **ELEVATOR** | ART DIRECTOR **TONY ADAMIC** | DESIGNER **TONY ADAMIC** | CLIENT **NADALINA**
PAPER/MATERIALS **MUNKEN PRINT WHITE 115 GSM, AND 300 GSM**

CROATIA

JKACZMAREK, FALLON | ART DIRECTOR **JESSE KACZMAREK** | DESIGNER **JESSE KACZMAREK** | CLIENT **EARL JEANS** | ★

★ | **JKACZMAREK, FALLON** | ART DIRECTOR **JESSE KACZMAREK, CRAIG DUFFNEY**
DESIGNER **JESSE KACZMAREK, CRAIG DUFFNEY** | CLIENT **EARL JEANS**

USA

S DESIGN INC. | ART DIRECTOR **SARAH SEARS** | DESIGNER **CARA SANDERS ROBB** | CLIENT **CABA** ★
PAPER/MATERIALS **MOHAWK SUPERFINE**

relationships.

options.

solutions

caba

relationships. options. solutions

options.

Options. While most people enjoy picking from several, too many options can be overwhelming and can hamper sound, informed decision making. Selecting and creating a benefits plan that best suits your company's needs requires the elimination of incompatible options. Affordability, ongoing changes in healthcare, legal compliance and retirement desires must be matched with the wide variety of available products.

By listening to your needs and identifying the viable and cost-effective options, we can present you with a plan that is consistent with your company's identity and management goals. Analyzing your specific needs, considering all factors including cost and legal requirements, leads to a simple, logical plan that reflects your company's ideals.

You can select the most appropriate benefit program, confident that you have considered all relevant possibilities.

★ | **SK+G ADVERTISING** | ART DIRECTOR **ERIC STEIN, STEVE AVERITT, MIKE MIGLIOZZI** | DESIGNER **HARRY FOREHAND, CHRISTINE TOSTI, ALEX SMITH, KURT SNIDER, BELLE LARSON, CARRI HALL, RAYNA LEE** | CLIENT **PLANET HOLLYWOOD RESORT, LAS VEGAS** | PAPER/MATERIALS **STERLING 100 LB. COVER, FOUR-COLOR PROCESS, EIGHT SPOT COLORS, SPOT VARNISHES**

VAIN (n.) van- ... ...ense of extreme pride in one's appearance or abilities, often supported by excessive adoration by the modest. ie: Some people are better looking than everyone else. That's a fact. Why should they pretend like they're not? That's not vanity. It's just the plain truth.

★ | **SK+G ADVERTISING** | ART DIRECTOR **STEVE AVERITT, PHILIPP BATALLIA** | DESIGNER **TRACY BROCKHOUSE, BORIS KOSTOV**
CLIENT **FOUR SEASONS OCEAN RESIDENCES** | PAPER/MATERIALS **MOHAWK NAVAHO 65 LB. COVER, SUEDE TEX, YUPO**

USA

SK+G ADVERTISING | ART DIRECTOR **JEREMY BRISTOL, CLAYTON JAMES, ERIC STEIN**
DESIGNER **KURT SNIDER, DIANDRE JOHNSON, MARSHALL AUNE, VANESSA ADAO** | CLIENT **ECHELON, LAS VEGAS**
PAPER/MATERIALS **UTOPIA PREMIUM GLOSS, 100 LB. COVER, FOUR-COLOR PROCESS, FOUR SPOT COLORS, AND SPOT VARNISH**

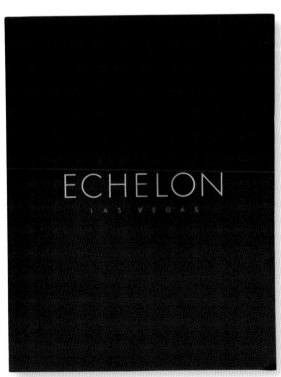

USA

★ | **ENV DESIGN** | ART DIRECTOR **JONAS GROSSMANN** | DESIGNER **JONAS GROSSMANN** | CLIENT **ZEPHYR**

GERMANY

FOLK CREATIVE MARKETING | ART DIRECTOR **ANDREW JENKINSON** | DESIGNER **SIMON HILL** | CLIENT **HIGHLAND**
PAPER/MATERIALS **SILK**

How would you describe
the architectural objectives
of The Levels?

The Levels was conceived principally as a response
to the urban context within which the building sits.
The principle corner is utilised as the basis for a six
storey architectural statement corner of glass and
coloured panelling, in order to create a strong urban
form and give the building a distinct character.
Going away from the corner the building steps down
in response to the adjoining buildings and takes a simpler
formal approach to follow the architectural precedent set
by the adjoining buildings.

The overall development consists of 54 apartments with
318 sq m of commercial space on the ground floor fronting
Hills Road. There is a separate block of 16 social housing
units, with an independent access from Homerton Street,
75% of which are reserved for key workers. Access to the
rear courtyard for parking is exclusive to the 38 private
apartments.

Internally the apartments are carefully designed taking
advantage of the light and views to create interesting
spaces with a variety of layouts.

Security is paramount at The Levels and from the
moment you enter the electronic gates we have done
everything possible to guarantee you peace of mind.
The Levels sits in harmony with its surroundings
whilst adding colour, contrast and focus to the local
cityscape.

A living space. The most
valuable commodity in the
world is space. Here at The
Levels, whether indoors or
outdoors, space is abundant.
We want you to make the
most of it.

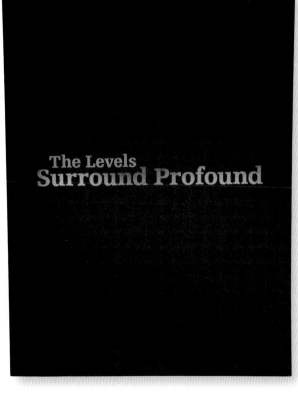

The Levels
Surround Profound

UNITED KINGDOM

★ **BANDUJO ADVERTISING AND DESIGN** | ART DIRECTOR **RYOSUKE MATSUMOTO** | CLIENT **GREENBERG TRAURIG, LLP**
PAPER/MATERIALS **MOHAWK NAVAJO BRILLIANT WHITE 65 LB. TEXT, 130 LB. DOUBLE THICK, EXTRA SMOOTH COVER**

BANDUJO ADVERTISING AND DESIGN | ART DIRECTOR **ROBERT BROTHERS** | CLIENT **CITI SMITH BARNEY**
PAPER/MATERIALS **MOHAWK NAVAJO BRILLIANT WHITE 120 LB. DOUBLE WEIGHT COVER, 100 LB. TEXT**

USA

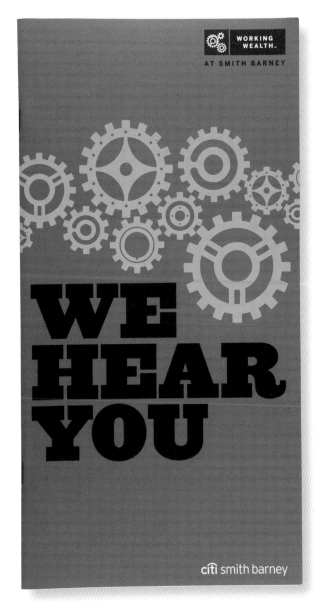

★ **CHASE DESIGN GROUP, INC.** | ART DIRECTOR **MARGO CHASE** | DESIGNER **AMY TSUI, TATIANA REDIN, BRIAN HUNT**
CLIENT **CARTOON NETWORK** | PAPER/MATERIALS **TOPKOTE COVER**

USA

CHASE DESIGN GROUP, INC. │ ART DIRECTOR **MARGO CHASE** │ DESIGNER **STEPHANIE RUBIN, MARIA GAVIRRIA,** ★
CLARK GOOLSBY, AMÉLIE BONET │ CLIENT **CARTOON NETWORK** │ PAPER/MATERIALS **MCCOY SILK TEXT**

★ **MILTON GLASER, INC.** | ART DIRECTOR **MILTON GLASER** | DESIGNER **DEBORAH ADLER** | CLIENT **SUNY STONYBROOK**
PAPER/MATERIALS **80 LB. MOHAWK TRUE WHITE SMOOTH COVER, 70 LB. MOHAWK TRUE WHITE VELLUM TEXT**

USA

FIFTY YEARS

THE EMERGENCE
OF STONY BROOK

FIFTY FACTS

EUROPE'S GREAT SCHOOLS took a leisurely millennium or so to achieve their greatness. In America, justly famed universities earned that fame slowly, over two or three centuries. So imagine the tiny ripple in academia, 50 years ago, when a nondescript college was born in a sleepy Long Island village. Its name is Stony Brook. And oh, what those 50 swift years have wrought.

FACT
13

IF NOT A MIRACLE…what would you call it? A machine chopped off both of Arsenio Matias's hands…and a team of doctors, nurses, and technicians at Stony Brook University Hospital reattached not one…but both of them.

FACT
14

DON'T LAUGH. If you can jingle your keys, maybe you're a budding Beethoven. In our Electronic Media Lab, you can transform those jingles into bite-size digital pieces, and turn them into beautiful music.

13

FACT
22

BY THE SEA, BY THE SEA. Stony Brook is now the only SUNY school with a campus on the Atlantic Ocean. It happened when we acquired Southampton College. We're embracing the new student body (and waves are hugging the shore).

FACT
21

WOW! Successful heart surgery! Nothing special about that, you say? Well, how about if the pregnant patient gives birth to triplets just before her heart operation? It really happened. At Stony Brook University Hospital. And all four are doing just fine.

21   22

★

USA

★ | **SAATCHI DESIGN** | ART DIRECTOR **KEVIN FINN, JULIAN MELHUISH** | CLIENT **SPICERS PAPER**

AUSTRALIA

ACTUALLY,
YOU'RE
HOLDING IT.

SPLENDORGEL.
STRANGE NAME.
SERIOUS PAPER.

So, IF THEY'RE
HOLDING THE LAST
BROCHURE, WHAT'S
NEW WITH
SPLENDORGEL?...

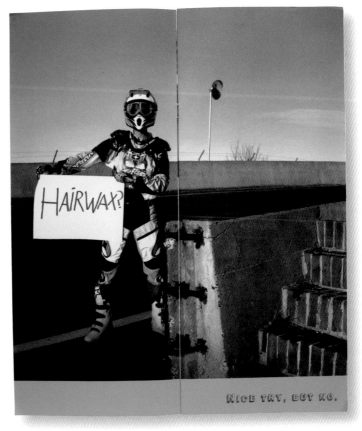

HAIRWAX?

NICE TRY, BUT NO.

★ **EBD** | ART DIRECTOR **ELLEN BRUSS** | DESIGNER **JORGE LAMORA, CHARLES CARPENTER**
CLIENT **ZI LOFTS AND TOWNHOMES** | PAPER/MATERIALS **NEENAH CLASSIC CREST AND TINTED SPOT VARNISH**

USA

NEO DESIGN | ART DIRECTOR **CRAIG HUTTON** | DESIGNER **CRAIG HUTTON, PAUL HOLLINGWORTH**
CLIENT **CONCEPT PERSONNEL** | PAPER/MATERIALS **COVER: SUPER BUFF, 350 GSM, TEXT: CHALLENGER OFFSET, 150 GSM**

★ | **JOHNSTON DUFFY** | ART DIRECTOR **MARTIN DUFFY** | DESIGNER **MARTIN DUFFY** | CLIENT **THE W GROUP**
PAPER/MATERIALS **SCHEUFELEN PHOENIXMOTION**

USA

JOHNSTON DUFFY | ART DIRECTOR **MARTIN DUFFY** | DESIGNER **MARTIN DUFFY** | CLIENT **WONDERBOY CLOTHING** | ★
PAPER/MATERIALS **DIAMOND SILK TEXT, MOHAWK SUPERFINE**

USA

★ | **JOHNSTON DUFFY** | ART DIRECTOR **MARTIN DUFFY** | DESIGNER **MARTIN DUFFY** | CLIENT **WONDERBOY CLOTHING**
PAPER/MATERIALS **DIAMOND SILK, DULL AQUEOUS COATING**

USA

JOHNSTON DUFFY | ART DIRECTOR **MARTIN DUFFY** | DESIGNER **ANDY EVANS, MARTIN DUFFY** | ★
CLIENT **WONDERBOY CLOTHING** | PAPER/MATERIALS **SCHEUFELEN CONSORT ROYAL BRILLIANCE BLUE WHITE**

★ | **KOLEGRAM** | ART DIRECTOR **GONTRAN BLAIS** | DESIGNER **GONTRAN BLAIS** | CLIENT **BUNTIN REID**

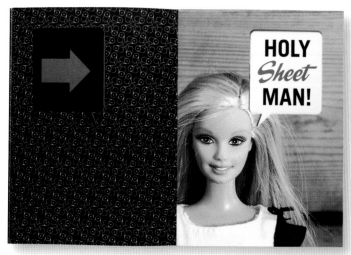

ROYCROFT DESIGN | ART DIRECTOR **JENNIFER ROYCROFT** | DESIGNER **JENNIFER ROYCROFT** | CLIENT **AQUENT** | ★

I've got twice the work, half the staff, and no budget to grow my team. | We launch one new product, and the next one's already rolling through the door. | We've got the marketing strategy. Now who can help us **We hear you** execute? | With so many audience segments, I need multiple executions of the same creative. Fast. | Our Web site looks great, but it's not generating enough revenue. | My customer base is constantly shifting. How do I learn what makes them tick?

AQUENT

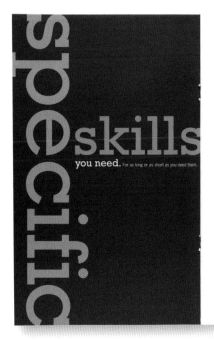

★ **CONNIE HWANG DESIGN** | ART DIRECTOR **CONNIE HWANG** | DESIGNER **CONNIE HWANG**
CLIENT **UNIVERSITY GALLERIES** | PAPER/MATERIALS **STERLING ULTRA GLOSS COVER, GILCLEAR**

SHINE ADVERTISING | ART DIRECTOR **MICHAEL KRIEFSKI** | DESIGNER **BRADLEY GUTTING**
CLIENT **AUBURN RIDGE** | PAPER/MATERIALS **COVER: GILBERT OXFORD SMOKED, TEXT: PHOENIX MOTION, XANTUR**

USA

★ | **THE CHASE** | ART DIRECTOR **STEPHEN ROYLE** | DESIGNER **STEPHEN ROYLE, LIZZIE CAMERON**
CLIENT **LAND SECURITIES**

UNITED KINGDOM

SLOVENIA

★ IN THIS SECTION

ARTS

★ **TOMATO KOŠIR S.P.** | ART DIRECTOR **TOMATO KOŠIR** | DESIGNER **TOMATO KOŠIR** | CLIENT **SLOVENIAN FILM FUND**
PAPER/MATERIALS **GARDA MATT WHITE, 120 & 300 GSM**

DESIGN ARMY | ART DIRECTOR **PUM LEFEBURE, JAKE LEFEBURE** | DESIGNER **MIKE MALUSO** ★
CLIENT **BLACK BOOK PUBLISHING** | PAPER/MATERIALS **HARD BOUND BOOK**

★ **WECHSLER** | ART DIRECTOR **MIKE HALL** | DESIGNER **MIKE HALL, AARON SHAW** | CLIENT **MUSEUM OF ARMY FLYING**

THE MUSEUM OF ARMY FLYING
Middle Wallop Stockbridge Hampshire SO20 8DY

★ | **RYSZARD BIENERT** | ART DIRECTOR **RYSZARD BIENERT** | DESIGNER **RYSZARD BIENERT** | CLIENT **GALERIA PIEKARY 5**
PAPER/MATERIALS **COVER: 3 MM CARDBOARD, SILKSCREEN PRINTED WITH METALLIC PANTONE, UV SPOT VARNISH, STEEL STAPLED, FINISHED WITH CANVAS SPINE**

POLAND

RYSZARD BIENERT | ART DIRECTOR **RYSZARD BIENERT** | DESIGNER **RYSZARD BIENERT** | CLIENT **MUZEUM ZIEMI LUBUSKIEJ**
PAPER/MATERIALS **COVER: DEBOSSING ON HANDMADE PAPER, INSIDE: COATED, UNCOATED STOCK, METALLIC PAPER**

POLAND

POLAND

SUBSTANCE151 | ART DIRECTOR **IDA CHEINMAN** | DESIGNER **IDA CHEINMAN, RICK SALZMAN**
CLIENT **ADVERTISING ASSOCIATION OF BALTIMORE** | PAPER/MATERIALS **FINCH FINE COVER AND TEXT, EMBOSSING**

★

USA

★ | **HANGAR 18 CREATIVE GROUP** | ART DIRECTOR **SEAN CARTER** | DESIGNER **TODD CHAPMAN** | CLIENT **UNISOURCE**

CANADA

HANGAR 18 CREATIVE GROUP | ART DIRECTOR **SEAN CARTER** | DESIGNER **TODD CHAPMAN** | CLIENT **UNISOURCE** | ★

INSPIRED. ORIGINAL. DETAILED. THOUGHTFUL. CRAFTED. SMART. INFLUENTIAL. Design that provokes, challenges, alters our expectations of what an annual report or brochure *should* be. Unisource is once again celebrating exceptional design work with NUARS 2007. INSPIRÉ. ORIGINAL. MINUTIEUX. RÉFLÉCHI. OUVRAGÉ. SOIGNÉ. INFLUENT. Design qui provoque, défie, change notre perception de ce que *devrait* être un rapport annuel ou une brochure. Unisource souligne de nouveau les projets de conception exceptionnels avec NUARS 2007.

THE RESEALED RESEALED

NU·ar^s

CREATIVE BRIEF

GREAT DESIGN

CHALLENGES EXPECTED THINKING.

THE 2007 NATIONAL UNISOURCE ANNUAL REPORT SHOW

NU·ar^s

CANADA

★ | **SAGMEISTER, INC.** | ART DIRECTOR **STEFAN SAGMEISTER** | DESIGNER **JOE SHOULDICE**
CLIENT **KUNSTHAUS BREGENT** | PAPER/MATERIALS **NEWSPRINT**

DESIGN ONE | ART DIRECTOR **JIM SLATTON** | DESIGNER **JIM SLATTON** | CLIENT **THE FURNITURE SOCIETY** | ★
PAPER/MATERIALS **COVER: ROYAL FIBER, 80 LB., TEXT: UTOPIA 2 MATTE 100 LB., 6" × 9" (15.2 × 22.9 cm) MYLAR BAG**

USA

MYRA PERRIN
Artist, Indianapolis, IN

3 Squared
Curly Maple, Bloodwood, Paint and Lacquer
7 x 20 x 9

I do mostly sculptural work, carved and painted.... this show allowed me to design something straight-forward, something simple, elegant and functional. I enjoyed going back to more traditional joinery and revisiting the exacting aspects of drawer making.

WILLIAM PICKFORD
Studio Furniture Maker, Rindge, NH

Offering
Mahogany, White Oak, Reclaimed Flooring and Ebony
40 x 28 x 18

This piece originated with a project at Rochester Institute of Technology that had to do with the source of inspiration for a drawer. I chose to focus on horror movies I had watched and I wanted to capture an eerie feeling on the exterior with an uplifting ending when you open the drawer. I have titled this piece *Offering* in hope that the viewer is able to take my concept and create their own narrative.

XXX $$ EXOTIC REVIEW
SHOW US YOUR DRAWERS
HOT! HOT! HOT! U ★★ 24 HOURS !!!

★ **AUFULDISH & WARRINER** | ART DIRECTOR **BOB AUFULDISH** | DESIGNER **BOB AUFULDISH, KATHERINE WARRINER**
CLIENT **SWA GROUP** | PAPER/MATERIALS **VARIOUS**

USA

DESIGNBOLAGET | ART DIRECTOR **CLAUS DUE** | DESIGNER **CLAUS DUE** | CLIENT **BAUM UND PFERDGARTEN**
PAPER/MATERIALS **UNCOATED PAPER**

DENMARK

★ | **AUFULDISH & WARRINER** | ART DIRECTOR **BOB AUFULDISH** | DESIGNER **BOB AUFULDISH, KATHERINE WARRINER**
CLIENT **SWA GROUP** | PAPER/MATERIALS **UNCOATED PAPER**

TOKY BRANDING + DESIGN | ART DIRECTOR **ERIC THOELKE** | DESIGNER **KATY FISCHER**
CLIENT **CONTEMPORARY ART MUSEUM, ST. LOUIS** ‖ ★

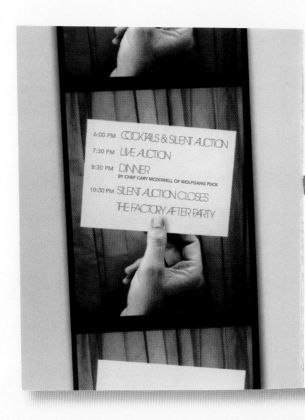

6:00 PM COCKTAILS & SILENT AUCTION

7:30 PM LIVE AUCTION

8:30 PM DINNER
BY CHEF CARY MCDOWELL OF WOLFGANG PUCK

10:30 PM SILENT AUCTION CLOSES

THE FACTORY AFTER PARTY

ARTS
THE ART
DESIRE
AND
WINE AUCTION

ON BEHALF OF THE BOARD OF DIRECTORS OF THE CONTEMPORARY ART MUSEUM ST. LOUIS, WE WELCOME YOU TO ARTS DESIRE: THE ART AND WINE AUCTION. THIS IS THE THIRD BIENNIAL AUCTION TO BENEFIT THE EXHIBITIONS AND EDUCATION PROGRAMS OF THE CONTEMPORARY, WHICH REACH THOUSANDS IN OUR COMMUNITY EACH YEAR.

The overwhelming generosity of artists and dealers in St. Louis – and in cities across the nation and around the globe – has been a truly moving indication that the art community is fully committed to furthering the success of the Contemporary Art Museum St. Louis. It is an incredibly generous gift to part with one's own creations, and we extend our deepest thanks to the artists who contributed to this outstanding Auction.

We are pleased to add an amazing Wine Auction to this year's lineup of events and are so thankful to the many wine collectors around the country who gave so generously. Special thanks to

★ **DESIGNBOLAGET** | ART DIRECTOR **CLAUS DUE** | DESIGNER **CLAUS DUE** | CLIENT **SUMO**
PAPER/MATERIALS **SLEEVE: CARDBOARD, TEXT: COATED PAPER**

PHOTOGRAPHERS

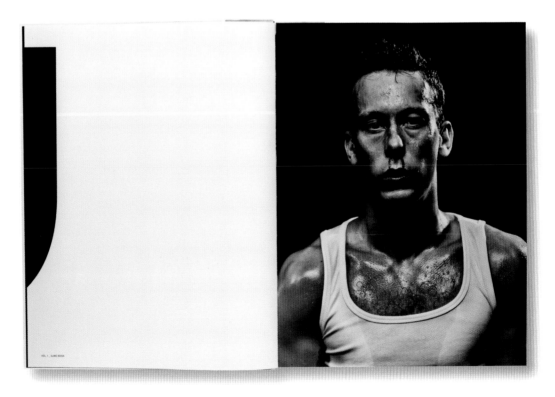

DENMARK

★ | **RIGSBY HULL** | ART DIRECTOR **THOMAS HULL, LANA RIGSBY** | DESIGNER **THOMAS HULL** | CLIENT **CAROL PIPER RUGS**
PAPER/MATERIALS **SCHEUFELEN PHOENIXMOTION**

USA

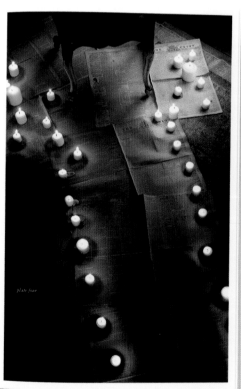

EBD | ART DIRECTOR **ELLEN BRUSS** | DESIGNER **JORGE LAMORA** | CLIENT **MUSEUM OF CONTEMPORARY ART, DENVER**
PAPER/MATERIALS **VELLUM SLEEVE**

★ **CONNIE HWANG DESIGN** | ART DIRECTOR **CONNIE HWANG** | DESIGNER **CONNIE HWANG**
CLIENT **UNIVERSITY GALLERIES** | PAPER/MATERIALS **MOHAWK SUPERFINE, EAMES**

USA

KARACTERS DESIGN GROUP | ART DIRECTOR **ERIC NIELSEN, JOHN FURNEAUX** | DESIGNER **ERIN HEALEY, CHRISTINA PINTO**
CLIENT **RGD ONTARIO** | PAPER/MATERIALS **WEYERHAEUSER COUGAR OPAQUE**

★ **LUKAS HUFFMAN** | ART DIRECTOR **LUKAS HUFFMAN** | DESIGNER **LUKAS HUFFMAN** | CLIENT **PULP PUBLISHING**
PAPER/MATERIALS **COVER: IRIS BROADCLOTH WHITE, TEXT: 100 LB. ACCENT OPAQUE WHITE, 100 LB. TOPKOTE GLOSS
AND DULL BOOK WHITE, 80 LB., 100 LB. ACCENT VELLUM BOOK WHITE, ENDSHEETS: 100 LB. ACCENT OPAQUE WHITE**

It'scrowdss
flashesfans
graphsatte
complime
ousexhi
richfortur
eternalinte
dangerous
tiveconfusi
revealingp
insecurete
tisticaldelu
lonely. It's

Could I have your autograph, please?

★ **DESIGN ARMY** | ART DIRECTOR **PUM LEFEBURE, JAKE LEFEBURE** | DESIGNER **DAN ADLER**
CLIENT **SIGNATURE THEATRE** | PAPER/MATERIALS **FINCH FINE**

USA

DESIGN ARMY | ART DIRECTOR **PUM LEFEBURE, JAKE LEFEBURE** | DESIGNER **DAN ADLER**
CLIENT **SIGNATURE THEATRE** | PAPER/MATERIALS **FINCH FINE, CARNIVAL LINEN, DIE CUT JACKET, FOIL STAMPING**

★ IN THIS SECTION

SELF-
PROMOTIONAL

★ **RETHINK** | CREATIVE DIRECTOR **IAN GRAIS, CHRIS STAPLES** | DESIGNER **ISABELLE SWIDERSKI, STEVE PINTER**
CLIENT **CAPIC** | PAPER/MATERIALS **100 LB. PRODUCTOLITH MATTE COVER, 100 LB. PRODUCTOLITH GLOSS TEXT**

CANADA

BILLY BLUE CREATIVE | ART DIRECTOR **JUSTIN SMITH** | DESIGNER **JUSTIN SMITH** | CLIENT **BILLY BLUE GROUP** | ★

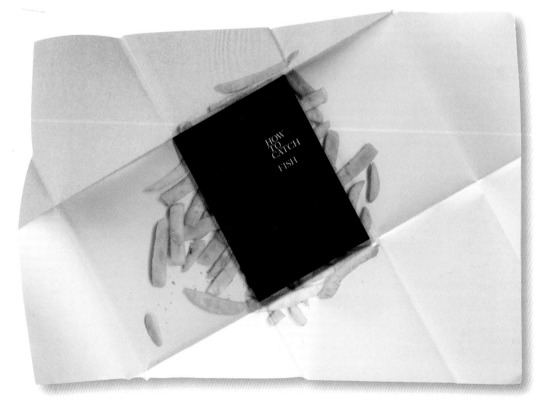

★ | **KYM ABRAMS DESIGN** | ART DIRECTOR **KYM ABRAMS** | DESIGNER **MELISSA DEPASQUALE**
CLIENT **ERIKSON INSTITUTE** | PAPER/MATERIALS **MOHAWK SUPERFINE**

USA

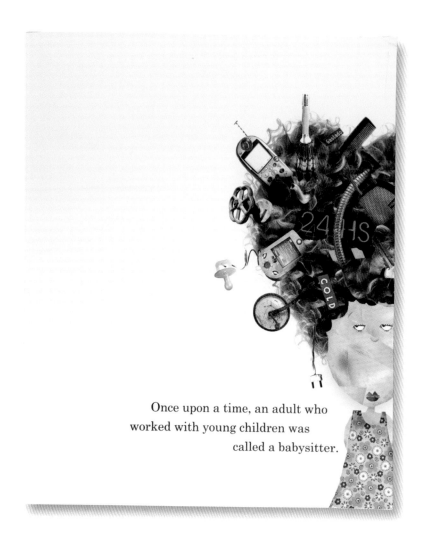

Once upon a time, an adult who worked with young children was called a babysitter.

GDC—GUGLIELMINO DESIGN CO. | ART DIRECTOR **SID GUGLIELMINO** | DESIGNER **JAMES BELL** ★
CLIENT **GDC—GUGLIELMINO DESIGN CO.** | PAPER/MATERIALS **NOVATECH SATIN AND CROMATICO EXTRA WHITE**

AUSTRALIA

yellow
gives clarity of thought, increases awareness, and stimulates interest and curiosity
yellow energy is related to the ability to perceive and understand

★ **CREATIVE SPARK** | ART DIRECTOR **NEIL MARRA** | DESIGNER **ANDY MALLALIEU** | CLIENT **OZ PROMOTIONS**
PAPER/MATERIALS **COVER: 350 GSM GLOSS, TEXT: 250 GSM UNCOATED OFFSET**

UNITED KINGDOM

WALLACE CHURCH, INC. | ART DIRECTOR **STAN CHURCH** | DESIGNER **JHOMY IRRAZABA**
CLIENT **WALLACE CHURCH, INC.**

★

USA

★ **GRAPHICULTURE** | ART DIRECTOR **CHERYL WATSON, LINDSEY GICE** | DESIGNER **CHERYL WATSON, LINDSEY GICE**
CLIENT **GRAPHICULTURE**

USA

MIRKO ILIĆ CORP. | ART DIRECTOR **MIRKO ILIĆ** | DESIGNER **MIRKO ILIĆ** | CLIENT **TIHANY DESIGN** | ★

★ | **LLOYDS GRAPHIC DESIGN LTD.** | ART DIRECTOR **ALEXANDER LLOYD** | DESIGNER **ALEXANDER LLOYD**
CLIENT **LLOYDS GRAPHIC DESIGN LTD.** | PAPER/MATERIALS **MATTE STOCK, 216 GSM**

NEW ZEALAND

LLOYDS GRAPHIC DESIGN LTD. | ART DIRECTOR **ALEXANDER LLOYD** | DESIGNER **ALEXANDER LLOYD**
CLIENT **LLOYDS GRAPHIC DESIGN LTD.** | PAPER/MATERIALS **MATTE STOCK, 216 GSM**

★

NEW ZEALAND

★ **PROPELLER** | ART DIRECTOR **DEE FRIEDMAN, ANDI SPEEDY** | DESIGNER **EMILY CARROLL, ANGELA PANIZA**
CLIENT **PROPELLER**

USA

LISKA + ASSOCIATES | ART DIRECTOR **STEVE LISKA, KIM FRY** | DESIGNER **KIM FRY, CAROLE MASSE**
CLIENT **LISKA + ASSOCIATES** | PAPER/MATERIALS **120 LB. MCCOY GLOSS COVER, 100 LB. MCCOY GLOSS TEXT**

CHICAGO
BOARD
OPTIONS
EXCHANGE
2005
ANNUAL
REPORT

Chicago Board Options Exchange 2005 Annual Report   Rebecca Taylor Print Advertising

rebecca taylor

Liska + Associates Inc. Communication Design   06 > 07

DAVID CARTER DESIGN ASSOCIATES | ART DIRECTOR **DONNA ALDRIDGE** | DESIGNER **LAUREN BERNDT**
CLIENT **SUSAN KAE GRANT BROCHURE** | PAPER/MATERIALS **PLIKE, SCHEUFELEN, GLAMA, SILKSCREEN, O-RING BINDING**

USA

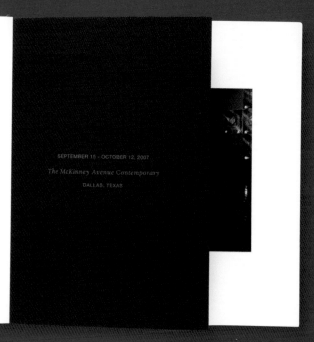

THIELEN DESIGNS, INC. | ART DIRECTOR **TONY THIELEN** | DESIGNER **TONY THIELEN** | CLIENT **THIELEN DESIGNS**
PAPER/MATERIALS **PERFECT BOUND, DIGITAL PRINTING, SCREEN PRINTED CARDBOARD**

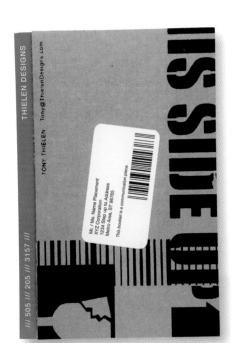

EMPLOYEE OF THE MONTH

MANY FIRMS DOWNPLAY AWARD SHOWS AND PUBLICATIONS. NOT US. WE CONSTANTLY SUBMIT WORK. WE FEEL IT'S IMPORTANT FOR BOTH CLIENTS AND PROSPECTIVE CLIENTS TO KNOW THAT WE DO MORE THAN JUST MEET INDUSTRY STANDARDS. WE EXCEED THEM.

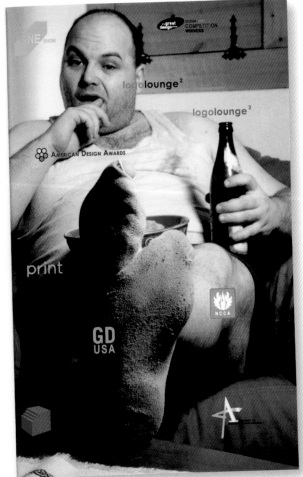

★ | **IE DESIGN + COMMUNICATIONS** | ART DIRECTOR **MARCIE CARSON** | DESIGNER **MARCIE CARSON**
CLIENT **IE DESIGN + COMMUNICATIONS** | PAPER/MATERIALS **MOHAWK NAVAJO, STRATHMORE WRITING, TOPKOTE GLOSS**

USA

SAGMEISTER, INC. | ART DIRECTOR **STEFAN SAGMEISTER** | DESIGNER **RADU RANGA** | CLIENT **ANNI KUAN DESIGN**
PAPER/MATERIALS **NEWSPRINT**

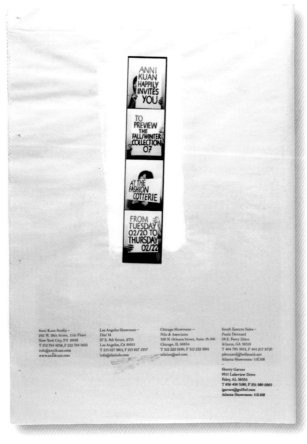

★ | **ANNABELLE GOULD DESIGN** | ART DIRECTOR **ANNABELLE GOULD** | DESIGNER **ANNABELLE GOULD**
CLIENT **DIGITALKITCHEN** | PAPER/MATERIALS **MCCOY**

USA

NEO DESIGN | ART DIRECTOR **CRAIG HUTTON** | DESIGNER **CRAIG HUTTON** | CLIENT **ALEX TELFER PHOTOGRAPHY** | ★

★ IN THIS SECTION

BANDUJO ADVERTISING AND DESIGN

THE JUPITER DRAWING ROOM

PHILOGRAPHICA, INC.

MIRIELLO GRAFICO

SAGMEISTER, INC.

TOKY BRANDING + DESIGN

EDUCATIONAL AND NONPROFIT

★ | **BANDUJO ADVERTISING AND DESIGN** | ART DIRECTOR **RYOSUKE MATSUMOTO** | CLIENT **THE FRENCH CULINARY INSTITUTE-** PAPER/MATERIALS **MOHAWK NAVAJO BRILLIANT WHITE 120 LB. COVER, 80 LB. TEXT**

USA

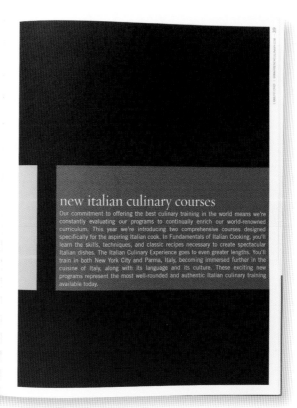

THE JUPITER DRAWING ROOM | DESIGNER **CARLA KREUSER** | CLIENT **INTERACTIVE AFRICA DESIGN INDABA 10**
PAPER/MATERIALS **AVALON MATTE**

PHILOGRAPHICA, INC. | ART DIRECTOR **DAVID HORTON** | DESIGNER **AMY LEBOW**
CLIENT **DEXTER/SOUTHFIELD SCHOOL** | PAPER/MATERIALS **COVER: MOHAWK VIA VELLUM, TEXT: SAPPI MCCOY MATTE**

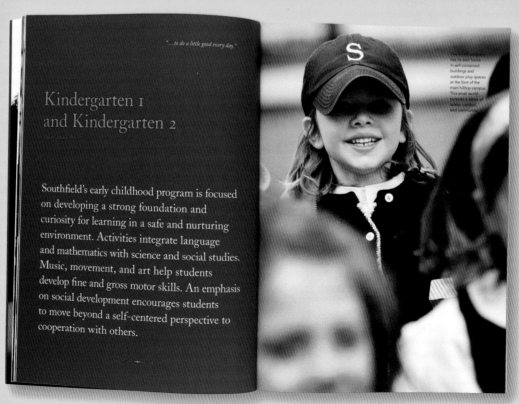

PHILOGRAPHICA, INC. | ART DIRECTOR **DAVID HORTON** | DESIGNER **AMY LEBOW** ★
CLIENT **DEXTER/SOUTHFIELD SCHOOL** | PAPER/MATERIALS **COVER: MOHAWK VIA VELLUM, TEXT: SAPPI MCCOY MATTE**

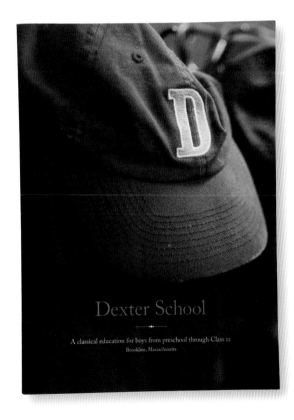

USA

★ **MIRIELLO GRAFICO** | ART DIRECTOR **DENNIS GARCIA** | DESIGNER **DENNIS GARCIA** | CLIENT **SCRIPPS RESEARCH INSTITUTE**
PAPER/MATERIALS **LUSTRO DULL MATTE**

SAGMEISTER, INC. | ART DIRECTOR **STEFAN SAGMEISTER** | DESIGNER **MATTHIAS ERSTBERWER**
CLIENT **COLUMBIA UNIVERSITY** | PAPER/MATERIALS **80 GSM MATTE COATED ART PAPER**

USA

★ **SAGMEISTER, INC.** | ART DIRECTOR **STEFAN SAGMEISTER** | DESIGNER **MATTHIAS ERSTBERWER** | CLIENT **ONE VOICE**
PAPER/MATERIALS **SAPPI COATED**

TOKY BRANDING + DESIGN │ ART DIRECTOR **ERIC THOELKE** │ DESIGNER **TRAVIS BROWN** │ CLIENT **ECOURBAN**
PAPER/MATERIALS **RUBBER BAND, BAMBOO, RAGLAN BAG**

DIRECTORY

112–118 50,000 FEET INC.
1700 WEST IRVING PARK ROAD
SUITE 110
CHICAGO, IL 60613
USA
WWW.50000FEET.COM

208 ANNABELLE GOULD DESIGN
7540 MARY AVENUE NW
SEATTLE, WA 98117
USA
WWW.AGOULD.COM
ANNABELLE@AGOULD.COM

176 AUFULDISH & WARRINER
183 THE ALAMEDA
SAN ANSELMO, CA 94960
USA
WWW.AUFWAR.COM
BOB@AUFWAR.COM

142 BANDUJO ADVERTISING AND DESIGN
143 22 WEST 19TH STREET, 9TH FLOOR
212 NEW YORK, NY 10011
USA
WWW.BANDUJO.COM

193 BILLY BLUE CREATIVE
52 LAMBERT ROAD, FLAT 3
LONDON
UK
WWW.BILLYBLUE.COM.AU
JUSTIN@FISHASSOCIATES.COM.AU

036 BLIK
055 655 G STREET, SUITE E
SAN DIEGO, CA 92101
USA
WWW.TYLERBLIK.COM
TYLER@TYLERBLIK.COM

044 BOCCALATTE
507/55 HOLT STREET
SURRY HILLS
SYDNEY, NSW 2010
AUSTRALIA
WWW.BOCCALATTE.COM

107 BONBON LONDON
F5, 13 THE PARAGON
LONDON SE3 0PA
UK
MARK@BONBONLONDON.COM

083–085 BRANDEX
STE. EAST 15 CHESTERFIELD PLACE
NORTH VANCOUVER, BC V7M 353
CANADA
WWW.BRANDFX.CA
SAMANTHA@BRANDFX.CA

086–094 BURTON SNOWBOARDS/SYNDICATE
80 INDUSTRIAL PARKWAY
BURLINGTON, VT 05401
USA
WWW.BURTON.COM

081 CAMPBELL FISHER DESIGN
5013 EAST WASHINGTON STREET, #230
PHOENIX, AZ 85034
USA
WWW.THINKCFD.COM
ER@THINKCFD.COM

014–015 CARRÉNOIR ROMA
028–029 VIA TATA GIOVANNI, 8
ROME 00154
ITALY
WWW.CARRENOIR.IT

057 THE CHASE
160 22 NEWMAN STREET
LONDON W1T 1PH
UK
WWW.THECHASE.CO.UK
STEVE.ROYLE@THECHASE.CO.UK

144–145 CHASE DESIGN GROUP
2019 RIVERSIDE DRIVE
LOS ANGELES, CA 90039
USA
WWW.CHASEDESIGNGROUP.COM

158 CONNIE HWANG DESIGN
185 815 5TH STREET
GAINESVILLE, FL 32601
USA
WWW.CONNIEHWANGDESIGN.COM

095 CREATIVE SPARK
196 116 BURY NEW ROAD
WHITEFIELD, MANCHESTER M45 6AD
UK
WWW.CREATIVESPARK.CO.UK
ANDY@CREATIVESPARK.CO.UK

204 DAVID CARTER DESIGN ASSOCIATES
4112 SWISS AVENUE
DALLAS, TX 75204
USA
WWW.DCADESIGN.COM

096 DECKER DESIGN
14 WEST 23RD STREET, FLOOR 3
NEW YORK, NY 10010
USA
WWW.DECKERDESIGN.COM
COURTNEYC@DECKERDESIGN.COM

108 DEI CREATIVE
159 WESTERN AVENUE WEST, SUITE 450
SEATTLE, WA 98119
USA
WWW.DEICREATIVE.COM

008–009 DESIGN ARMY
030 510 H STREET, NW #200
070–071 WASHINGTON, DC 20002
165 USA
188–189 WWW.DESIGNARMY.COM
PUM@DESIGNARMY.COM

012 DESIGN CENTER LTD.
026–027 KNEZOVA 30
LJUBLJANA SI 1000
SLOVENIA
WWW.CEHOVIN.COM
RUSSIA
OPETRUSHIHA@DESIGNDEPOT.RU

175 DESIGN ONE
53 ASHELAND AVENUE, SUITE 103
ASHEVILLE, NC 28801
USA
WWW.D1INC.COM
175

097–101 DESIGN RANCH
103–105 1600 SUMMIT
126 KANSAS CITY, MO 64108
USA
WWW.DESIGN-RANCH.COM
IS@DESIGN-RANCH.COM

128–129 DESIGNBOLAGET
130–131 RYESGADE 3F, 2ND FLOOR
177–178 2200 COPENHAGEN N
180–181 DENMARK
WWW.DESIGNBOLAGET.DK
DUE@DESIGNBOLAGET.DK

043 DIE TRANSFORMER
IMMERMANNSTASSE 39
44147 DORTMUND/NRW
GERMANY
WWW.DIE-TRANSFORMER.DE

132 ELEVATOR
B. BERISSLAVICA 1
SPLIT 21000
CROATIA
WWW.ELEVATOR.HR

061 EBD
150 2500 WALNUT STREET, #401
183 DENVER, CO 80205
USA
JORGE@EBD.COM

140 ENV DESIGN
ARCHENER STREET 82–84
50674 COLOGNE
GERMANY
WWW.ENV-DESIGN.COM

141 FOLK CREATIVE MARKETING
2A LUKE STREET
LONDON EC2A 4NT
UK
WWW.FOLK.UK.COM
MARK@FOLK.UK.COM

182 GDC—GUGLIELMINO DESIGN CO.
195 33 BAXTER STREET
FORTITUDE VALLEY
BRISBANE, QLD 4006
AUSTRALIA
WWW.GDESIGN.COM.AU
THEPEOPLE@GDESIGN.COM.AU

198 GRAPHICULTURE
22 1ST AVENUE NORTH, 5TH FLOOR
MINNEAPOLIS, MN 55401
USA
WWW.GRAPHICCULTURE.COM

016 HANGAR 18 CREATIVE GROUP
106 220–137 WEST 3RD AVENUE
172–173 VANCOUVER, BC V6J 1K7
CANADA
WWW.HANGAR18CREATIVE.COM

038 HELENA SEO DESIGN
102 1000 ESCALON AVENUE, SUITE 1012
SUNNYVALE, CA 94085
USA
WWW.HELENASEO.COM

206 IE DESIGN + COMMUNICATIONS
422 PACIFIC COAST HIGHWAY
HERMOSA BEACH, CA 90254
USA
WWW.IEDESIGN.COM
KENNY@IEDESIGN.COM

133–134 JKACZMAREK
209 WEST 13TH STREET, #4
NEW YORK, NY 10011
USA
INFO@JKACZMAREK.COM

152–155 JOHNSTON DUFFY
803 SOUTH 4TH STREET, 1ST FLOOR
PHILADELPHIA, PA 19147
USA
MARTIN@JOHNSTONDUFFY.COM

018 THE JUPITER DRAWING ROOM
033–034 3RD FLOOR THE TERRACES
213 BLACKRIVER PARK OBSERVATORY
CAPE TOWN
SOUTH AFRICA
AROSS@JUPITERCT.CO.ZA

067 KARACTERS DESIGN GROUP
185 1600, 777 HORNBY STREET
VANCOUVER, BC V6Z 2T3
CANADA
WWW.KARACTERS.COM
TIM.HOFFPANIR@KARACTERS.COM

045 KIMIKO CHAN DESIGN
2030 3RD STREET, LOFT 10
SAN FRANCISCO, CA 94107
USA
KIMIKO@KIMIKOCHANDESIGN.COM

156 KOLEGRAM
37 ST. JOSEPH BOULEVARD
GATINEAU, QUEBEC J8Y 3V8
CANADA
WWW.KOLEGRAM.COM

123–124 KORN DESIGN
116 SAINT BOTOLPH STREET
BOSTON, MA 02115
USA
WWW.KORNDESIGN.COM
FERNANDO@KORNDESIGN.COM

194 KYM ABRAMS DESIGN
213 WEST INSTITUTE PLACE, SUITE 608
CHICAGO, IL 60610
USA
WWW.KAD.COM
MELISSAD@KAD.COM

About the author

Over the past fifteen years, Perry Chua has applied his strategic thinking to clean, compelling, innovative designs. Although he sees the true reward of his work in the success of his clients, Chua has collected his share of awards from international entities including Applied Arts Awards and Summit International Awards, among others. Chua's work has been featured in over a dozen Rockport Publishers graphic design books, a Barcelona design journal, and a Boston University design textbook titled *Fundamentals of Graphic Design* (Laurence King Publishing, London).

Throughout his career, Chua has developed innovative brand design systems for many clients including McDonald's Restaurants, Mountain Equipment Co-op, Four Seasons Private Residences, Intrawest ULC, and Nokia.

Chua currently resides in Vancouver, Canada, with his wife Lori and their two adorable children. He is the design director at Spring Advertising and Design, and a part-time brand-design instructor at Vancouver Film School.

Chua is also the coauthor of Rockport Publishers' *Logo Savvy: Top Brand-Design Firms Share Their Naming and Identity Strategies*, released in March 2007 and available in bookstores worldwide.